Uncertain Times
A Chief Investment Officer's Journey

Uncertain Times
A Chief Investment Officer's Journey

By Alton R. Cogert, CFA, CPA, CAIA

CB Woodbridge Publishing

Copyright © 2009 by Alton R. Cogert, CFA, CPA, CAIA. All rights reserved

Published by CB Woodbridge Publishing.

All rights reserved. No part of this publication may be reproduced, stored in a retrieval system, or transmitted in any form or by any means, electronic, mechanical, photocopying, recording, scanning or otherwise, except as permitted under Section 107 or 108 of the 1976 United States Copyright Act, without the prior written permission of the Author. Requests to the Author for permission should be addressed to Alton R. Cogert, CFA, CPA, CAIA, President and Chief Executive Officer, Strategic Asset Alliance, 11 Bellwether Way, Ste. 209, Bellingham, WA 98225.

Cover and Interior Design: Stripe Graphics Ltd.
Richmond, B.C., Canada V7E 4Z2

Limits of Liability/Disclaimer of Warranty: While the publisher and author have used their best efforts in preparing this book, they make no representations or warranties with respect to the accuracy or completeness of the contents of this book and specifically disclaim any implied warranties of merchantability or fitness for a particular purpose. No warranty may be created or extended by sales representatives or written sales materials. The advice and strategies contained herein may not be suitable for your situation. You should consult with a professional where appropriate. Neither the publisher nor the author shall be liable for any loss of profit or any other commercial damages, including but not limited to special, incidental, consequential or other damages.

The story of the Chief Investment Officer's journey is fictional. Names, characters, businesses, organizations, places, events and incidents either are the product of the author's and/or his collaborator's imagination or are used fictitiously. Any resemblance to actual persons, living or dead, events or locales is entirely coincidental.

First print edition, November, 2009.
Printed and bound in the United States of America.

ISBN 1-4392-5918-6
LLCN 2009909738

For LeeAnn and Kathryn

ACKNOWLEDGEMENTS

Thank you for taking time from your busy day to embark on this journey with our Chief Investment Officer friend. This book is not designed to be the definitive text about investment processes for insurance companies. Rather, it presents key aspects of the process in an easy to read and, I trust, an enjoyable and understandable context.

Uncertain Times also reflects influences, in varying degrees, of many people who have guided me over the years. That especially includes those with whom I have come into contact and everyone with whom I have had the pleasure to work during the fifteen year life, to date, of Strategic Asset Alliance. I remain honored to have met every one of you and I thank you for your impact on the constant improvement at our firm.

However, in writing this book, I would especially like to thank a few special people, without whom *Uncertain Times* would not have been published. Thank you to my collaborator, Robert Fripp, of The Impact Group, Toronto, Canada. And, thank you to Sharon Atkins, Strategic Asset Alliance's former Marketing Director, who introduced me to Mr. Fripp and provided constant friendly reminders of "How's the book going?" Also, there would be no Strategic Asset Alliance without the efforts of my co-founder Gordon Coomans. Thank you, Gordon. I hope you enjoy this book.

Most importantly, I must thank my father, who provided an entrepreneurial inspiration and my mother, who showed me how to laugh at the absurdities of the world.

I save a final thank you for one of my grandparents, Charles Bragin, who kept trying to impart basic wisdom to my brother, sister and me. As a child, I never quite understood why he would say, "Do you want to be a big fish in a little pond, or a little fish in a big pond?" Thank you, Grandpa. I think I finally figured it out.

A.C.

INTRODUCTION

This is the story of someone you may know. Or, you may know someone in a similar situation. Or, it just might be about someone like you.

Uncertain Times tells the story of a Chief Investment Officer (CIO) employed by an insurance company, who must find a way to cope in today's economy.

Way back in March, 2008, I wrote in my blog, *From the Northwest Quadrant*, about "The Greatest Deleveraging in the History of the World" (www.saai.com/index.php/2008/03/). I wrote that we had discussed several key issues at our firm's client-only conference, but that this single topic seemed to be the most important.

Indeed, since then, the "Greatest Deleveraging" has hit the United States and global economies with a vengeance, bringing wrenching changes not only to financial markets, but to the communities and lives of people throughout the world.

Insurance companies, as you know, pay their policyholders' claims for insurable events. For property/casualty companies, that might involve an auto accident, fire, legal judgment, and so on. For life/health companies, the insurable event is usually a death, disability or health-related expense claim, but it can also be as simple as a request from a policyholder for funds from his or her annuity account. These claims are paid only after the policyholder has paid a premium to an insurer to bear the risk of that event occurring.

Of course, policyholders do not make claims immediately after they pay premiums, so their insurers have the duty to invest their premium dollars prudently, awaiting future use.

In the current environment, insurance senior management teams and Boards of Directors are coping with the severe problems one reads about in the financial press, but from their own unique perspective. Most insurers thought they were in the insurance business and that just having a 'conservative' investment philosophy would serve them well, allowing them to focus on insurance instead of investment issues.

However, financial markets have changed dramatically in the last twelve months and what was considered a 'conservative' approach has now been proven not to be. What should those companies do now? How should they react? Where do they start? I wrote this book to help those senior management and Board members deal successfully with these 'uncertain times.'

One thing is certain about investing: a solid process gives you the best opportunity to produce solid results. Good results may occur in spite of an inadequate process, but that may be attributable to a degree of luck. Though there are no guarantees, solid investment results will most likely follow from a solid investment process.

We define the investment process as a series of seven major interrelated activities, called the Investment Process Value Chain. Each of these activities provides an opportunity to add or subtract value.

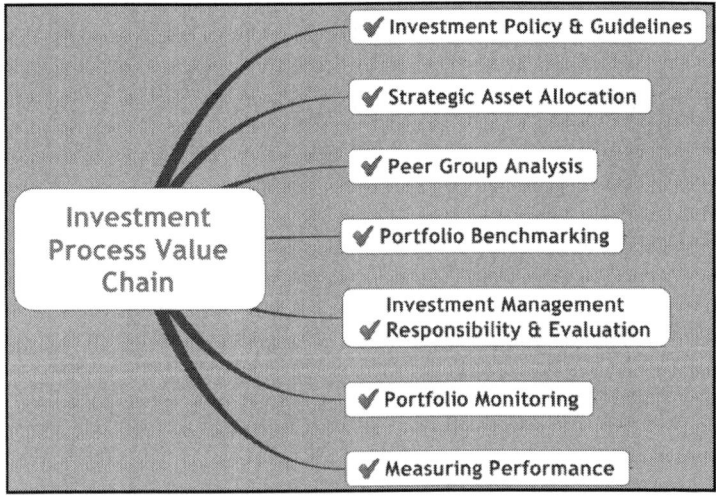

Uncertain Times **considers these in detail, thus:**

- **Chapter 4**, *Steering the Investment Portfolio to Success*, discusses Investment Policy and Guidelines.
- **Chapter 3** considers *Decisions, Decisions: Strategic Asset Allocation: The Investment Cornerstone*.
- **Chapter 5** takes on Peer Group Analysis, under the title, *Mirror, Mirror On the Wall, Am I Comparing Myself to the Best or the Worst?*
- *To Chop or to Stretch? The Little Matter of Portfolio Benchmarking*, and its impact on the process, is our topic in **Chapter 6**.
- **Chapter 7** tackles issues surrounding the actual management of assets under the title, *Whose Call is it Anyway? Investment Management, Responsibility and Evaluation*.
- **Chapter 8** considers Portfolio Monitoring in *Don't Close Your Eyes! Keep Your Portfolio on a Short Leash*.
- And **Chapter 9**, *Performance Measurement, A Not So Simple Task,* weighs in on a topic that is far more complex than it appears.
- Finally, because even the best investment process can be mishandled, **Chapter 2** tackles perhaps the most important topic of them all in, *Communication, Communication, Communication*.

You will find that the question: 'How can one develop the best possible investment process for an insurance company?' involves a much more complex process than simply 'Get me the best yield or return for my money.'

The complexity of the answers to that question is something that our CIO friend confronts as we discuss our industry's challenges—and his. For, you see, *Uncertain Times* is more than an interesting tale about an insurance company's CIO. It will guide you when you confront these situations while answering the key question: How can I develop the best possible investment process for an insurer? For more information on this and related issues, I invite you to discover the book's website and related blog at www.uncertain-times.com.

I hope you enjoy reading about our CIO's journey in 'uncertain times'; and that it brings to your personal journey a renewed dedication to improve your company's investment process.

Alton R. Cogert, CFA, CPA, CAIA
President and Chief Executive Officer
Strategic Asset Alliance
Bellingham, WA
www.saai.com

TABLE OF CONTENTS

CHAPTER 1 An End is a Beginning 1
Notes 5

CHAPTER 2 Communication, Communication, Communication 11
Notes 23

CHAPTER 3 Decisions, Decisions. Strategic Asset Allocation 29
Notes 37

CHAPTER 4 Steering the Investment Portfolio to Success 53
Notes 65

CHAPTER 5 Mirror, Mirror on the Wall, Peer Group Analysis:
Am I Comparing Myself To the Best or the Worst? 77
Notes 89

CHAPTER 6 To Chop or to Stretch?
The Little Matter of Portfolio Benchmarking 105
Notes 117

CHAPTER 7 Whose Call is it, Anyway?
Investment Management, Responsibility and Evaluation 127
Notes 139

CHAPTER 8 Don't Close Your Eyes,
Keep Your Portfolio on a Short Leash 153
Notes 167

CHAPTER 9 Performance Measurement,
A Not So Simple Task 181
Notes 197

CHAPTER 10 Onwards and Upwards 213

CHAPTER 11 Epilogue 225

INDEX 227

1

AN END IS A BEGINNING

He couldn't believe it. He had just been fired! Robert E. Short was the Chief Investment Officer for a medium sized insurance company—or rather, he had been. He had thought his work was well respected. Two months earlier his CEO had slapped him on the shoulder, asserting, "You've got a bright future with us, Bob." Fast forward to two minutes ago. Voices in the hall and a knock on his door. Sixty seconds later he was unemployed. It was that quick.

Jim Greening, the Chief Financial Officer, was still talking across the desk. He'd said what he had come to say, and now he had the nerve to smile. Couldn't the man summon the courtesy to shut his mouth and walk away? Bob tried to listen, but the shock of the moment left him battle-deaf, mute. He tried to concentrate, but his mind kept drifting off—to Iraq, of all places. And that was nearly twenty years ago!

Staring at Greening's face, Bob was aware that his brain was blocking the other's words. The odd thing was the flashback that replaced them. He was seeing himself in the hatch of his M2A2 Bradley Fighting Vehicle. The night was wonderfully clear and he was moving at speed over the rough desert surface of sun-split rocks while the hatch's steel rim punched his ribs black and blue.

In 1991 Bob had been a young officer commanding a unit in the 24th Mechanized Infantry Division assigned to Desert Storm. To the left of them the French 6th Light Armored Division; to the right, the British 1st Armored Division. The combined Allied force had been ordered to attack into Iraq early on Sunday, February 24, 1991, from a point just west of Kuwait. Their wing formed part of the "left-hook" intended to knock out the Iraqi 45th Infantry Division before swinging east for a flanking attack on Saddam Hussein's Republican Guard.

It was the French who hit the Iraqi 45th that night; it was the French who took the casualties.

"So that's it, Bob. Times are tough and we have to hone our investment side to this department's full potential." Bob surfaced intermittently, listening to Greening's words in equal parts shock, disbelief and fear. "I'm afraid you're not the man to lead us forward here. We need someone more aggressive." Bob recognized the fear in himself as he listened. He had known it before his unit had started to roll. It had seemed to dissipate the moment his Bradley's wheels began to churn. [SEE NOTE 1-1]

Bob was looking at Greening, but thinking about Susan. She had quit work before their child was born, and they had a year-old baby daughter to support. Without an income. The thought didn't last. The starry orb of an Iraqi night eclipsed even his family from Bob's mind.

Out in the desert, armed with the sophistication of modern weaponry, he had needed neither compass nor GPS. The vehicles advancing in line abreast behind him were driving through a storm of sand and grit churned by the leaders; but Bob, in the front line, was running in the clear. For minutes on end that night he could have charted their course by the North Star. West Point had taught him advanced electronics, battle tactics, command techniques—and celestial navigation for survival.

Across the desk Greening was saying, "…a chance to refresh your skills, Bob." Then came the word "lacking," and "Maybe you should take more courses in communication. We could arrange that in your outplacement package."

Maybe, Bob told himself, he should have been a history teacher. The Academy's Department of History (Motto: "Wisdom Through History") had been the source of his favorite courses.

The moment the 24th Mechanized got its fighting orders, a glance at the map had told him their heading would put them on course for Cunaxa. Twenty-four centuries earlier the brothers Cyrus and Artaxerxes had battled each other at Cunaxa to rule the Persian Empire. Artaxerxes lost the battle; Cyrus lost his life, leaving 10,000 Greek mercenaries stranded in enemy territory far from home. One of those men, Xenophon, survived to write a book that still figured in leadership courses. At least, it did at West Point. It was no coincidence that Bob had taken Xenophon's *Anabasis* to Iraq, even—so it seemed as they roared through the night—into battle. At forty miles an hour on rough terrain the M2A2 Bradley's diesel was designed to keep pace with an M1 Abrams battle tank. Bob had stuffed several books in his jacket pockets that night, Xenophon's *Anabasis* among them, to pad the blows from the rim of the Bradley's hatch.

Across the desk, Greening was wrapping up. "I'm glad we had this conversation, Bob." Improbably, the VP advanced his hand and Bob shook it, dazed. "When you're ready to do the paperwork, see Martha in HR. She's got it waiting."

She's got it waiting! How long had this ambush lain in store, ready to be sprung?

Bob sat a moment, feeling for all the world as Xenophon must have done, a man marooned a thousand miles behind enemy lines, very far from home. [SEE NOTE 1-2]

It was time to act. Bob packed his family photos and his personal files, turned off his computer and the Bloomberg monitor, dropped his keys and left. Security would do the rest. The CEO's recently voiced line, "You've got a bright future with us, Bob," would have to happen elsewhere.

The 24th Mechanized Infantry never reached Cunaxa. The French disengaged from the smoking remains of the Iraqi 45th Infantry and the whole line wheeled right, the Americans and British slowing to maintain the Allies' arcing line abreast to attack the Republican Guard. That didn't happen. The Guard joined the general Iraqi retreat, where Allied aircraft bombed men and materiel to destruction on the "Highway of Death." Three days later Bob's U.S. 24th Infantry played a major role in the battle at Rumailah (the battle of the junkyard), hammering Republican Guard vehicles into the sand. That was where Bob tasted fear again, keeping one eye on the sky. The Air Force killed more "friendlies" than Iraqis did.

Eighteen years earlier, Lt. Robert S. Short had done his bit to win a bigger battle than he faced now. He could do it again. He must. As he escaped the building he was once again keeping his eye on a metaphorical sky—avoiding the most familiar faces. He made it to the parking lot and the refuge of his car, wondering what to tell his wife. He reasoned that Susan might not be surprised. She knew that her husband was bright, but his communication skills were another matter.

That had been the brunt of Greening's criticism.

Bob toyed with his car key. How had his apparent failures short-changed the company? Greening had listed other factors to justify dismissing him but Bob had been too shell-shocked to take it in. No matter. He'd piece it together. He had to before he could move on.

1
CHAPTER NOTES

What does the story of Bob Short have to do with investing for insurance companies?

NOTE 1-1

What does the story of Bob Short have to do with investing for insurance companies?

Whether you have worked for an insurer, are currently doing so, or may do so in the future, parts of Short's story may sound familiar. In fact, it plays an integral part in learning about how best to organize and execute the investment process for an insurer.

Short works—I should say 'worked'—for a medium-sized insurer, so some of his challenges may be too simple compared to those you face. However, the basic challenges are here, and you will have to confront them successfully if you are to provide the best possible investment results for the insurer.

So, how does one develop a successful investment process?

An excellent question. And one that we deal with every day as investment consultants for insurance companies. You should know that our firm, Strategic Asset Alliance, is the only investment consulting company serving the insurance industry exclusively. We don't manage assets, but we help companies to improve their investment process with a focus on improving their financial results. You can find more information about us, as well as information that can assist in improving your company's investment process at our web site (www.saai.com).

NOTE 1-1

You will get the benefit of Short's experience in this book, of course, but you will also get the benefit of the perspectives from our firm, whose principals are all former Chief Investment Officers of insurers, and who have collectively been responsible for over $30 billion in assets.

So, back to our key question: How to develop a successful investment process?

Start with the 'end result' in mind.

What is your priority? Portfolio yield, total return, no realized losses, or something else?

We submit that the investment portfolio of an insurer exists primarily to support the business of that insurer. The portfolio would not exist without the insurance business written, and being held, as reserves to cover future claims, losses, surrenders, etc.

And, the portfolio would also not exist without the capital (raised or accumulated over time) in the company. It is there for a reason—to provide shareholders (or policyholders in the case of a mutual company) with a fair return. But, the desired return would never come about without a successful insurance business.

So, first and foremost, it is important to keep the role of the Chief Investment Officer in perspective. It is a vital position within corporate senior

NOTE 1-1

management. It exists to serve the goals and objectives of the company.

What is the 'end result' then? For many insurers, it is not portfolio yield or total return; it is return on surplus (shareholders' equity), net income, earnings per share, or another similar measure tied to the overall financial performance of the company. We call these measures 'key performance indicators' (KPI) of success.

Corporate goals and objectives are tied to the desired KPIs over a given time period. It follows that the investment process must have a series of goals and objectives directly related to achieving that end result.

For example, if Short's company wants return on surplus, he should fully understand the accounting ramifications of how return on surplus is calculated, and how the investment portfolio contributes to that.

For an insurer, such a KPI usually means a fixed income portfolio focused on investment income as well as total return, and an equity portfolio (if applicable) focused on total return. Importantly, investment income should be viewed net of credit impairments, an increasingly difficulty issue from both an economic and accounting perspective.

Many times, we see companies whose investment goals are disconnected from corporate KPIs to some degree. That can pose an underlying problem that festers until the two really do diverge significantly. This can result in a series of unintended consequences.

NOTE 1-2

Consider the environment Bob faced during 2008. Equities down over 40%. Supposedly safe fixed income investments buffeted by a near total lack of liquidity, and pricing that expects the worst in defaults and then some. Mortgage-backed securities that would pay in full, corporate bonds that were the pillars of the economy, and other 'rock solid' investments all valued at 'fire sale' prices.

On top of that, we found auditors effectively calling the shots on what must be written down as 'Other Than Temporarily Impaired' and pushing the dangerous standards of 'fair value' found in 'mark to market' accounting. Meanwhile, rating agencies, running scared from their own problems, delve into investment portfolios as much to salvage their own reputations as to understand the risks in the portfolio.

To this, we can add senior management and a Board of Directors stunned that a 'conservative' portfolio can get into trouble so quickly. If all the above factors wouldn't make Bob Short feel marooned, it most surely made many other CIO's feel that way—even without the added pressure presented to Short at the beginning of our story.

2

COMMUNICATION, COMMUNICATION, COMMUNICATION

He was hissing with anger, hissing at his wife, hissing at the world. Once he had come close to kicking Molly, their dog. Bob even had to force himself to sit in his own small study. Without a job and a paycheck, his desk, chair, computer, even the little room itself were meaningless! The seeming permanence and security of his surroundings mocked him.

"Bob, Bob, Bob, calm down." Susan stood behind him, bending over him where he sat in his office chair, her arms around him, holding him as tightly as she could until his fit of anger passed. "Bob, this isn't the end!" She used the swivel action of the chair to rock him back and forth, back and forth. "Bob, it's just a setback. Honey, more than ever we need you to be you!"

"Let go of me, Sue! I can't breathe. I gotta get out of here!"

This had happened before. On those occasions he had used the swivel to his own advantage, roughly pushing away her embrace, storming out of the house to walk for miles.

Sue could hear Sarah crying, but the baby was safe in her playpen. Gambling, she used all her strength to keep her husband clamped in his chair. "Bob, we went through this before. It didn't help. You can walk out of your room, or out of our house, but *you* can't walk out of you! Honey, calm down! Please, Bob, you're hurting my wrists." Still she clung on. Some of the force seemed to have drained from him. He wasn't using his strength against her. Some impediment seemed to have passed.

"Damn! Damn! Damn! Damn!" This time he escaped her clutch, but it was only to push himself forward and down on the desk, his head between his arms.

"Honey," she told him quietly, "it's O.K. to cry."

"I'm not crying, Sue! That was anger. That was real grief. There's gotta be a better world out there!"

"Of course there is. You don't have to work for those…"

"Shits!"

"You told me weeks ago the company was sinking, Bob. Let it go!"

"Benchmarks! What do those clowns know about benchmarks?"

"They'll soon find out what they didn't know." Susan could feel his body shaking with anger.

"People come in, they take over a solid company and the very next day my returns are no good, my portfolio stinks, I'm slacking because I set my benchmarks too low…"

"Bob, don't torture yourself."

"…Low benchmarks! It means I'm being too cautious; and it's hunting season on my judgment, from equity to equity…"

"Stop it!"

"…from bond to bond. It went on for months!"

"I know that. I watched them tearing you apart."

"That bastard Greening…"

"He's going to be next. And he knows it. He can't print cash." Sue paused to let the message sink in. "But you know something? What's worse than watching *them* tear you apart is watching *you* tear you apart!"

Bob was calmer now. The fight was out of him. "It's like the emperor's clothes," he told her through his elbow. "You know what they're doing? They're robbing the books to pay for their takeover. The cash wasn't there the day before they took over. They knew that. Why should it be there the day after? But you have to play along. A million bucks? No problem, Boss. I'll get another million overnight."

"Bob!"

"Bastards!"

"Bob, listen to me!"

"Huh?"

"If you'd had officers like that in the Army, you'd probably be dead!"

That thought stopped him cold. "Too true! You're right!" Bob pushed himself up, which made Sue realize she was still holding him down.

"Here!" he said.

"What do you want me to do with that?" she asked.

"I put this bookmark in last night. I want you to read that!"

"Xenophon, Bob?"

"Yes."

"Why?" Sue asked, in genuine surprise.

"Because the old rascal always seems to fit."

Sue pushed her long, straight hair aside to see the page. "Why," she read, "being more sinned against than sinning, need we rob ourselves, too?"

"D'you see what I mean?" he asked her.

"D'you see what I mean?" she fired back.

"What?"

"They're out of your life. They can't hurt you any more."

UNCERTAIN TIMES | 13

She waited until his shoulders stopped heaving. "Congratulations!"

"What for?"

"You won back your self-respect!"

Repair took time, but it was only a matter of days before Bob snapped out of the worst of it and gained a grip on his self-control. It was Sue, still huddling with Bob at his office desk, who had found the next line, the one after "being more sinned against than sinning." She read it triumphantly: "We know the measure of discipline!" And he did.

Within weeks, Bob was teaching nights at the business school of his local state college. He had drafted a proposal, adding highlights for a nine-part course and full teaching notes for the first of his proposed classes. His topic: "Investment strategies: Strategic asset allocation for corporate revenues—Introduction." Teaching evenings at a business school was not his preferred career option, but his specialty fit the curriculum. Seeing potential, the academic director was prepared to give the course a chance to grow from a nucleus of just three students. Bob appreciated the gesture: his course must run at a loss. The academic director supplied a short, handwritten list of names:

1. Sally Prentice, started as realtor, then personal finance. Says she wants a "bigger" career. Single mom.
2. Ken Stiller, grad. from Chicago School Econ. (Milton Friedman's school. Monetarist) Ken is dept. comptroller for a dept of state government.
3. Bill Hanna. Insurance agent. Says he wants to "come over to the other side."

The evening of his first class Bob managed to cover his nerves well for a guy who couldn't communicate.

"Let's make this as interactive as possible," he told his

students. "By the way, the course description mentions allocating *corporate* revenues. I'm going to teach this course from a better perspective than that: we're going to talk about revenues held by insurance companies. The difference is that large insurance companies need to generate cash-flow from their invested revenues to pay out claims, so they tend to be extra sophisticated when it comes to strategic asset allocation."

No one responded.

"If it's just me dumping on you, you'll miss the benefit of this course. What's important is you relating to the problems you're going to face. The best way to get there is to discuss what happens and what you'll confront every day. I want you to bounce ideas off me and I'll bounce them back. Everyone fine with that?"

He could have heard a pin drop.

"If that's a vote of confidence we may as well quit now!"

"Sure. Let's bounce." Ken Stiller was a tall, lean graduate of the Chicago School of Economics, a prestigious alma mater. Stiller was working as an economic advisor to a department of state government.

"Good." Bob took a moment to remind himself of Jim Greening's parting advice: Take more courses in communication. It was true; he had never been the most communicative of men, a trait that years in the Army hierarchy had only emphasized. He started to speak, feeling caught in a lie.

"Front and center in this course we're going to talk *Communication*. When you land a job as an investment officer with an insurance company you'll find that every one of the people you have to deal with has a 'need to know' claim on what you do. Your company's financial health depends on it."

Stiller shot back, "Communication is a buzz word…"

"Say that in a job interview and you lose it right there!" Bob's quick repartee commanded attention. Nobody spoke.

He tried conciliation. "You're right. Communication is a

buzz word. It also happens to be essential if you're at the center of the web, which is where—since you're taking this course—you want to be."

Stiller again: "Corporate communication departments *announce* decisions. They don't *make* 'em."

"We're on a higher level, Ken. Long before anyone announces anything, the effective policy decisions are made high up the line by senior managers, and that's the *result* of extensive communication. That's where we're at."

"That's P.R.-speak for 'stakeholder input.' "

"Sure. It also happens to be real world-speak. You don't get good stakeholder input unless you ask the right people the right high-level, high-knowledge questions. Senior managers focus on communications at the *front* end of decision-making. Look, by the end of this course I hope to prove to you that a good communication policy equals good leadership."

Sally Prentice cut in, "I read somewhere that the higher the rank of a corporate officer, the more time that person spends on pure communication."

Bob nodded. [SEE NOTE 2-1]

"And C-suite people drive on high-beams. They're more future-oriented than the lower ranks." Sally was dressed in a smart black business suit, for a night-school course. She had "corporate potential" written all over.

She paused, giving Bob time to pick up: "If the word *communication* is a business school cliché, that's because it's critical. If it ever was a cliché, that ended in the Nineties when information technology shot holes through the concept of running large companies as vertical silos. Companies work up, down and sideways these days and I.T. has made life a whole lot easier in many respects, but it's no substitute for face to face." Bob amazed himself, talking like a born communicator! "You have to involve the troops." [SEE NOTE 2-2]

"You got that right!" A portly, middle-aged insurance agent,

Bill Hanna, was taking the course "to come over to the other side," as he put it, hoping to manage investment revenues instead of writing the insurance policies that would earn those returns. "No one ever sold insurance without perfecting their personal pitch."

"Don't limit yourself to one pitch here. The higher you go the more pitches you need for different stakeholders. Let me step back a minute, Bill…" Bob consulted his talking points and noticed he had skipped a line. "The key activity of an insurance company is to write, underwrite and sell insurance. That generates revenue we have to invest—a science in itself. I flatter myself that's why you're here: to learn how and where you invest, what investments to sell and when you will sell them. The investment decisions you make will be critical to the success or failure of an insurance company."

Bob watched with relief as his students took notes. On one level it proved they were alert to information that would help them tweak their CVs for prospective employers. On another level, important to Bob, it meant they were hearing things worth taking down.

"The fact is—you'll know this, Bill—the insurance business is so competitive there's not much room to make money by writing insurance alone. If your company is going to make profits, they may have to accrue from investment decisions you make. Your investments have to make sense."

Bob had never fancied himself a public speaker, but now he held their full attention. He plowed on, gaining confidence.

"You guys want jobs in the hot seat! Anyone heard the term *combined ratio*?"

"Does it mean profit and loss?"

"Not quite, Sally, but you're close. In general terms, if your losses and expenses for claims are *more* than one hundred percent of the insurance premiums or revenues coming in, then we say your combined ratio is over 100%." Bob wrote that figure on the white board, adding the mouth of a sad face in one of the zeroes. "That's bad. You have to sell investments to make up the difference." He waited a moment, then wrote the same figure again. "If you're actually making money on insurance, then your combined ratio is under 100% and you're plowing revenues into the investment side." This time he drew the smile of a happy face. "That's good."

The white board had their attention. Bob took advantage of raised eyes. "I said investment officers need great communication skills. Why?"

"You have to consult a lot of people?" ventured Bill.

"Yep. Can you be specific?"

"You're talking to brokers?" Answers still came as questions. Not surprising. The introduction was the most general part of the course. At this point the information-set supporting the jobs these people hoped to get came from all quarters.

"More to the point, you're talking to analysts. But let's leave them aside. Who else?"

"Managers."

"O.K., let's be specific. The marketing side is generating premium payments. That's either the company's agents or independent agencies. The managers are on the insurance side, and your people are into investments. The insurance side is sending you revenue, if you're lucky, or it fell on its face and needs cash. Either way, cash-flow is moving through your sphere of responsibility, coming in or going out." Bob warmed to his task. "You're the investment officer, the center of the operation, trying to satisfy the what, the why, the how much and the when! You have to be talking to—and I don't just mean reporting to— your CEO, your CFO, accountants, analysts and managers.

"It's like that in any organization, but for a chief investment officer the communication challenge is larger than life. *You* are the one they expect to supply the cash! *You* are the one who needs to cultivate more points of contact than anyone else in the shop, because you have to let them know how you plan to support their insurance-related activity.

"Got it?" he asked. "In a real sense, it doesn't matter how many managers you have above you. What I'm telling you is subtle, but this is a fact." He drew out the words to stress them. "As long as *your* investment skills and *your* business-smarts are priming their pump, *you* are the leader, not the cashier."

Ken Stiller: "I bet it's tricky telling that to the power structure."

"You don't *tell* them. It's how you behave with them; it's how you *treat* them. Here's the difference." Bob moved to the podium as if to emphasize the importance of what he was about to say. "I'm not suggesting you say 'This is my baby. You'll get results, so go away!' You have to go out of your way to make it a team effort. Everyone across the operation has a personal stake in success on the investment side. Bring 'em all into your tent. They won't have your expertise—but one by one you bring them on board, inform them, keep them on side. That's where communication is important.

"Let me give you an example. We'll take something simple—and believe me, this is simple. Let's say your insurance company sells policies through agency sales people, whether it's owned by the company or an independent. Those agents want to work for companies that do a good job with all the money they're bringing in.

"So you have agents looking over your shoulder. They want to know: Do you have a lot of below-investment-grade bonds? Do you have problem investments? Who doesn't, these days? Full disclosure may hurt your stock price—and then you get grief from upstairs. But if you're a policy holder, or an agent, and you see these things, you get nervous. The first thing they're going to think is: Should I have my insurance with somebody else? So you have to keep at them. Look, you have to deal with people—keep up front with them on warnings, reassurances, your framework plans."

Bob turned away, ostensibly to wipe the board. He was sweating. He was expressing sentiments he had never practiced.

He turned back: "What you're doing is giving your stakeholders the power to warn and to advise, and by the way…"

Sally Prentice interrupted. "And you don't get to carry the can alone…"

"…when your plan gets pummeled by reality!" added Bill.

Bob stayed at the podium, smiling. "That's when spreading responsibility around has its advantages."

"What's that book got to do with investment tactics, Bob?" Ken Stiller pointed to the dog-eared book on the instructor's desk.

Embarrassed, Bob realized he had been riffling pages while he spoke. He had never taught a major course before: maybe the book was his security blanket. Quick on his feet he replied, deadpan, "What does Xenophon's *Anabasis* have to do with investing, and managing investments? Nothing, and everything."

He turned the book over to read the publisher's blurb on the back. "I brought it in because it's instructive," he told them. "Here's why." He began to read:

" 'With their senior officers killed by treachery, they pitted themselves against the hostile lands of the empire. Their only supplies were what they could win by the sword. The 'marching republic' of 10,000 survivors turned north, braving 500 miles of desert, mountain and wild country, even crossing the Tigris while under attack. The Ten Thousand made *ad hoc* decisions, voting in their leaders, tactics and destiny while they were encamped, surrounded or on the march.'

"It's those *ad hoc* decisions about 'leaders, tactics and destiny' you need to keep in mind!" Bob told his students. "When these mercenaries left Greece, the author of this book, Xenophon, was not an officer, not even a private. He was an Athenian gentlemen along for the ride—to do a bit of networking. When the bottom fell out, he persuaded the survivors to vote for his tactics and strategy, and brought them safely home. If you are going to run an investment department on which the fortunes of a company depend—especially through a recession—then Xenophon's character just might be what you should project!

"Try this scenario," he told them, as evenly as he could manage. "You may be doing a swell job one day, but then the company gets taken over and the raiders expect you to generate the cash to pay for it—out of the same investment pot! Good communication is at a premium. Apart from *anything* else—and I mean anything!—it's your best line of self-defense."

His students looked at each other while Bob wiped the board, signaling the end of class. His students could not know it, but Bob was experiencing a personal moment of epiphany! It hit him hard. In a flash he realized that, had he followed the advice he had just given his students, he might still have his job.

He turned to the class. "If you're going to be a senior investment officer you will have to become a leader—full time," he told them. "That doesn't mean making rash personal judgments. It means taking a level-headed approach to everyone in your shop. No fear, no favor. If you want to go where I've been," he added, "read the *Anabasis*. You'll make a great chief investment officer. You'll also learn survival skills." [SEE NOTE 2-3]

CHAPTER NOTES

A good CIO must also learn, instinctively, intuitively, and completely, that investments exist to support the insurance organization.

NOTE 2-1

Let's look at this point another way. In many cases, the higher the rank of a corporate officer, the less they truly understand the details...without fully admitting that, of course.

Businesses have become increasingly complex entities over time, and insurers are no exception. Perhaps the most important skills a CIO can have are not technical, not even the ability to 'call' financial markets correctly most of the time. Perhaps the most important skill is the ability to communicate clearly, gathering all the complexity of investing for insurers and expressing it in terms that others in the organization can fully understand and use to make decisions.

Let's repeat that: Perhaps the most important skill a CIO can have is the ability to communicate clearly...and convincingly. Investments and finance are not easy subjects for the non-expert to fully understand, since even experts disagree to some degree. Thus, the ability to teach humbly and effectively, while putting across key points, is both a basic and vital requirement for a CIO.

NOTE 2-2

We see many insurers who still run their business in silos. Perhaps to a lesser degree than a few years ago, but the silo approach still rears its head.

Can a company begin to improve its operations materially if it breaks down the silo structure that is so traditional within the management of insurance companies? We believe so because we have seen it time and time again. Furthermore, a company's CIO should be an active supporter, even an activist, of how best to dissolve silos and improve communications across the company.

Actuaries in a silo-based organization focus on reserve adequacy, product pricing, cash-flow testing and the like, all very vital functions. In many cases they have little time to express their communications in ways that make their analyses and conclusions easier to understand. It has also been said that the actuaries tend to make a basic set of assumptions about the investment portfolio and then expect the investment team to execute strategy around their assumptions. However, everyone knows that investing and marketing insurance are more complex than models assume. The actuaries can be a key ally in understanding risk across the entire organization, so they are most effective when working closely with the rest of the organization, making certain that everyone is on the same track from a financial perspective.

NOTE 2-2

The marketing group in a silo-based organization will focus on product sales, despite the profitability or relative lack of it generated by any given product. It has often been said that after senior management spends hours developing a commission system, the salespeople will spend many more hours learning how best to 'game' that system for their own benefit. This is not unexpected. Quite frankly, it is a sign of a motivated sales team—although motivations may differ from the company's. Importantly, the marketing group must spend time advising the rest of the senior management team about the customer/policyholder/agent. This group is closest to the company's Number One reason to exist—to insure policyholders. It is also the marketing people who can transform the actuarial group's assumptions into an insurance policy suited to the real world. Marketing can also advise as to how policyholders and agents are viewing the investment portfolio's risk level in these uncertain times.

The investment team in the silo-oriented organization sees its role as one of obtaining a given yield, or managing against a total return benchmark. If the investment team achieves the yield and/or return benchmarks,, then it considers itself successful, despite whatever is happening elsewhere in the organization. In fact, some organizations tie incentive compensation to beating those benchmarks, thinking little about how that might impact the insurer's overall financial results in the long and short run.

NOTE 2-2

Another thought: It is probably the investment team that is best placed to inject a discussion of risk appetite into the organization, since investments may be the easiest item on the insurer's balance sheet to model and analyze for risk/reward. A company should develop communications that account for actuarial, marketing and investment perspectives, at the same time combining those with the risk appetite of the Board and senior management. That is the first and foremost way an investment team can add value and transcend a typical silo organization.

In some organizations, this can be accomplished through the use of a risk management committee of some kind. We will discuss risk management or its related names of Enterprise Risk Management, Asset/Liability Management, or Dynamic Financial Analysis in Chapter 3.

NOTE 2-3

Not every CIO needs to develop his communication plans as if he and his company were fighting a war (although some days it may seem that way). However, a CIO must rapidly assert his or her importance in the senior management team by communicating and facilitating communications through all parts of that team. A good CIO must also learn, instinctively, intuitively, and completely, that investments exist to support the insurance organization. Those are the lessons the class in our story is learning here.

3

DECISIONS, DECISIONS

STRATEGIC ASSET ALLOCATION:
The Investment Cornerstone

Bob had never been good at taking notes. Perhaps that was part of his problem. But he started making them now. Alone in his study he had made several pages of notes already. Now he started adding bullet points:

- How did I determine the company's asset allocation?
- Compare to how I <u>should have</u> determined the company's allocation
- What biases did I build into my analysis?
- What could I have done differently?
- Would it have made a difference?

He was preparing for his next night-school course. And beyond. Maybe he could write the book on strategic asset allocation in investment strategy. That might give him powerful leverage towards a new job. [SEE NOTE 3-1]

"More coffee?"

Susan stood in the door, carafe in hand.

"No thank you, Sue. I must be floating in it!"

"What are you doing?"

"Well, on one level, making notes for class."

"On another level?"

"They're going to be more complete than I need for night-school. I must have plans, but I haven't figured them out."

"Let me guess: you're going to write a book!"

"Yes," he said, sheepishly, but spoiled the moment, adding, "Who'd want to buy a book from me?"

His wife put down the carafe and began to massage the muscles in Bob's shoulders. "Hey, no need for that! Did you know twenty-six publishers rejected John Grisham's manuscript for *A Time To Kill*? Twenty-seven publishers rejected Dr. Suess's first children's book. And nine threw out J.K. Rowling's first *Harry Potter* story."

"How d'you know that?"

"Because I'm unusually bright!" Sue giggled at her touch of self-mockery. "And because I read it on the book review page moments ago!"

Bob had decided, before he proposed, that Sue resembled a young Mary Tyler Moore, who kept the home fires burning in repeats of the *Dick Van Dyke Show*. His wife, though, showed a lot more down to earth logic and determination than the actress was allowed to express.

Sue bent forward to kiss Bob's cheek, and froze. "Why did you write that?"

"What?"

"That last bullet point!" Beneath the first five, Bob had written a final line. It read: Who gives a hoot!"

Sue completed her kiss, her long dark hair bobbing almost down to Bob's notepad. "Cross it out," she suggested, adding,

"Tear off the sheet and start again. You don't need that. You've only got five little lines. Copy them onto another page."

"You're right." Bob ripped off the offending sheet. It crumpled with a satisfying sound.

"That's better." Sue encouraged him, relieved: "Why don't you try your notes on me?" she prompted him gently. "I *did* start life as an accountant in investments with a degree in constitutional history. Bizarre, huh?"

"How could I forget? Let's sit over there." They moved to a short sofa and sat side by side.

Bob scribbled his five points again. She watched him add notes as he spoke. "As an investment officer with an insurance company the most important decisions you make have to do with the strategic asset allocation."

"I sort of know what that means," she told him. "But a lot of folks won't."

"It means, where do you place your investments, for how long, how do you divide them up and place them in different classes, how liquid are they, and what is your rate of return?"

"That's better. Go on."

"That's strategic asset allocation. You have to base your decisions on long-term relationships among assets of different classes…"

"Oh Bob! I'm sure it's important, but if you start like that your students will think you're speaking Greek. You have to work your way into difficult topics…"

"What do you mean? How would you start?"

"Put the key point simply. That's what's important."

"I tell you what. You can edit the notes—or the book when it's finished. Right now I'll just sort of spot ideas down on the page and talk them through."

"Good idea. Shoot!"

They were both sliding down on the sofa. An onlooker might think they were dating.

"On the investment side," said Bob, in a tone that suggested he was telling a bedtime story, "you have to make *all* your decisions from a single point of view. You're supporting the *insurance* business. That's it. And that's the first thing my students need to know. They have to base their decisions on getting answers to questions about the *insurance* side of the business. For example, what reserves do the insurance folks need if they're going to meet their liabilities to policy holders? How much do they need, and when?"

"Uh-huh."

"Sue, don't go to sleep!"

"I'm not. You said, 'You're supporting the *insurance* business. That's it!' Am I right?"

"You're right. On second thought, that's not the first question. The first question you want to ask about their policy-holder reserves is: what is the duration of those reserves?"

"You mean, how long will they last?"

Bob responded, surprised, "That's what I said."

Susan snuggled against him. "Keep it simple."

"I'm trying!"

"Go on."

"You ask yourself questions about estimated cash flows. How much do you need from the reserves versus the estimated cash flows your investments will generate?" [SEE NOTE 3-2]

Susan teased him. "I know where we're going."

"I bet you do, too. In three words, spell it out!"

Susan half turned towards Bob and they mimed: "Asset Liability Management."

"Let's have a drink," he suggested.

"Nah. Too late. How much do you have to do tonight?"

"Just this. There's ALM, Asset Liability Management; and DFA, dynamic financial analysis."

"You need to tell them the difference." Susan slipped off her shoes and wiggled her toes in the shag rug. "And you'd better tell me, too."

"They're similar, but if you're a *life* insurance company you use ALM. If you're a *property-casualty* company you'll go for DFA. What you want to do when you're developing an asset allocation is…"

"…sacrifice a prisoner of war!" she shot back suddenly.

"What?" Bob turned on Sue, incredulous.

"Bob, Honey, listen to yourself. You take yourself too seriously. I've been catching up on Xenophon. When your precious Greeks got stuck between a rock and a hard place they sacrificed a prisoner of war to examine his entrails."

He smiled. "I can think of some I'd like to sacrifice."

"Not tonight." Susan rubbed her feet in the shag rug. "Let's wrap it up!"

"O.K. I was saying, before I was so rudely interrupted…"

"Your preferred decision-making tool is a spreadsheet!" Susan clapped her hand over her mouth and gestured him to continue.

"What you want to do in working out an asset allocation is to look at both sides of the balance sheet. You need some analytics—that's the ALM or the DFA—to let you determine a range of outcomes on the liability, a range of cash flows, a range of statements, and…"

"…a range of balance sheets!" She looked at him mischievously. "How'd I do?"

"You got an A!" [SEE NOTE 3-3]

"Or you could look for spots on the liver. That's what Xenophon did."

Bob swatted his wife with a cushion. She had finally punctured his reserve.

"Things will come out all right, you know," she told him.

"I know." He bent down to retrieve his pen and she kissed the back of his neck.

"Why," she asked, "do you refer to that crazy book?"

He posed his responses as questions: "Because it played a formative part in my life? Because it's iconic in its way—about making decisions under extreme duress?"

"May I suggest?"

"Of course."

"Because you had a lucky war and a wonderful life—until now!"

"There's a lot of truth in that." He pulled her close and kissed her head. "Can I go on?"

"Of course. Keep making your mini-notes. We'll pick them up later."

"O.K., you have your outcomes on the liabilities from the insurance folks. Now you need a similar range of outcomes for the *investment* side, and how they all inter-react. For example, if you're a property-casualty insurer facing a load of claims, you might consider liquidating some investments."

"Liquidating." Sue was slouched down, smiling. Her eyes were closed.

"O.K. Selling! Better?"

"Much. It's amazing."

"What is?"

"The way I hear you tell it, a chief investment officer makes more decisions than a general or a CEO."

"It's the whole job," Bob replied. "Not just strategy, but tactics, too." Susan looked drowsy. Bob went on quietly, "You consider selling investments to meet the insurance people's claims. That has to be key in your decisions on the asset allocation side. On the other hand, if your company generates positive cash flows across the board, then your underwriting results are either just terrific or you're a growing company that looks set to grow for the next few years."

"If you're that lucky…" came a sleepy voice.

"If you're that lucky you can decide to invest with the idea that you won't have to draw on your investment portfolio."

"Decisions, decisions. The company hangs on your every deed. I'm proud of you, Bob."

He squeezed her hand. "One final point. If an insurance company has a surplus in excess of the reserves it keeps to meet liabilities…"

"That's the company's 'net worth' I'd guess." Behind her closed eyes Susan was still alert.

"Or 'shareholders' equity.' Terms like that, yes. You invest those funds in a variety of things: fixed-income securities, for starters. Other assets are typically equities: they could be convertibles, bonds or stock; they could be real estate investment trusts, REITs."

"The bigger the company, the more varied their options, I'd guess."

"Good point. Thanks, Sue. You could put 'em into venture capital, private equities or hedge funds. You name it."

"I hope you're making notes, Bob."

"Enough to write them up tomorrow," he assured her. "We're almost there. Usually when you look at strategic asset allocation you're looking for the best mix. You want to find two things. The first is risk. You have to decide how big you want your 'risky bucket' to be. That's the non-fixed income allocation," he added, glancing at the small desk clock. "How much of the non-fixed income surplus do you want to put at risk?"

"Is that it for tonight?"

"Hang in, Babe. That's the simple bit. Within that risky bucket, how do I want to invest?"

"Sounds like a song title." Her voice trailed off.

"It could be. It's a popular question. It all goes into the analysis. DFA and ALM can help, but when it's time for that risky bucket sort of efficient frontier, Markowitz-type analysis is going to help with that." [SEE NOTE 3-4]

Suddenly Susan was awake and shoving her shoes on her feet. "Now you did it! It's too late for efficient frontiers and

Harry Markowitz. Let's go to bed!"

"I think I know my first mistake," Bob mused.

Susan turned to him, fully alert. "Do you really? I want to know."

"Not listening enough. Doing my own thing. Not consulting." He shrugged. "You have to listen to their opinions. Even if you don't factor them in you still have to hear them." [SEE NOTE 3-5]

"You know the best thing about that approach?" she asked him earnestly.

"What?"

"If a lot of people have input into a bad decision, you don't carry the can alone."

"I did, didn't I."

"You did. Let it go. We can't go back. It's time for bed!"

3
CHAPTER NOTES

For some insurers, determining the 'optimal' strategic asset allocation can be like writing a detailed treatise...

NOTE 3-1

For some insurers, determining the 'optimal' strategic asset allocation can be like writing a detailed treatise—an overly complex process that never seems to end. And, for some, it could be as simple as 'just don't lose any money,' so invest in investment grade bonds and a little bit in stocks and we're done with that decision.

However neither approach is probably the best one for an insurer. Remember that insurance company investments exist to meet the obligations of the written insurance business as well as provide a solid long term return on surplus.

Thus, the first step an insurer should take is the establishment of an informal or formal group for the review of its investment strategy, taking into account both sides of the balance sheet, as well as future business. For many companies, the group is simply an investment committee made up of key senior management members. But, for other insurers, that group is an Asset/Liability Management (ALM), Enterprise Risk Management or similar committee with representatives not only from the investment area, but from actuarial, marketing and other key C-level parts of the company. Whatever direction the company takes on this, the committee must use analytical tools that consider both sides of the balance sheet, as well as future business, in developing the proper asset allocation strategy.

NOTE 3-1

For property/casualty companies the analytical tool would typically be called Dynamic Financial Analysis (DFA), while for life companies it would be called Asset/Liability Management (ALM). Both tools basically do the same job, but both tools have been subject to their own set of problems and, thus, ridicule by some.

You've probably heard statements like this from folks trying to understand and use DFA. (We'll use that as our catch-all term for both tools going forward):

- "That requires too much complex input to be worthwhile. Can't we get to a solid answer without all these actuarial details?"
- "That DFA software was built by actuaries for actuaries, which is all well and good until you have to explain how you got your results to a Board of Directors or the rest of senior management."
- "There are too many assumptions in the DFA model to make it worthwhile. Just change a few and you get a completely different answer, so what good are the results?"
- "We really don't have the staff time to dedicate to using DFA—and what good are the results going to be anyway?"
- "DFA software is way too expensive for something that just gives us a general idea of how to invest and provides only marginal benefits on any other decisions we might make."

NOTE 3-1

For many insurers, these complaints are appropriate. DFA is just a tool and results must be interpreted by us humans before they can begin to have any meaning. In fact, several insurers have spent seven figures and up trying to implement DFA and when they finally do the results are little used or understood. However, if the basics behind DFA are understood as well as the pitfalls in interpreting its results and there is a committee or group in the company that relies upon its analyses as a decision guide, the results can be quite useful.

For example, an insurer with a given portfolio duration may want to consider the cost/benefit of increasing the duration in an environment of an upward sloping yield curve. They might say, 'We'll get more yield, but we will be taking on more risk—is it worth it?' Although this may seem like an 'asset only' decision that would not need consideration of reserves (liabilities), we must once again go back to the purpose of insurance assets—to support the business of the insurer.

NOTE 3-1

DFA can do just that and help frame the problem numerically, showing the range of possible outcomes on measures like investment income, total return, net income or return on surplus.

For example, when considering increasing portfolio duration, an insurer may have long duration reserves which would favor the use of long duration assets. Conversely, shorter duration reserves might mean that a possible good 'asset only' decision of, for example, taking more interest rate risk for more yield, could actually produce a serious mismatch between assets and liabilities and result in more overall risk than the insurer can prudently bear.

And, that's just one of many situations where DFA can be successfully used to determine the 'optimal' asset allocation. In fact, let's take a look at some sample results from a DFA analysis.

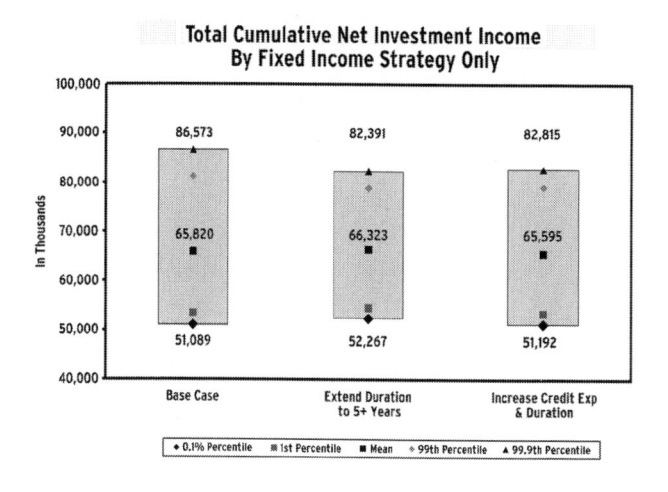

Total Cumulative Net Investment Income By Fixed Income Strategy Only (In Thousands)

Strategy	0.1% Percentile	1st Percentile	Mean	99th Percentile	99.9th Percentile
Base Case	51,089		65,820		86,573
Extend Duration to 5+ Years	52,267		66,323		82,391
Increase Credit Exp & Duration	51,192		65,595		82,815

UNCERTAIN TIMES | 41

NOTE 3-1

This is an example of a company looking for more yield by either increasing portfolio duration and/or adding credit risk. Notice the range of possible investment income for the base case (unchanged strategy) and for the other strategies being considered. If you think those boxes look about the same, you are correct. Remember, we are talking about a model that is designed to approximate reality, not provide 100% accurate results. Although the company's senior management thought that adding interest rate or credit risk could be one way to gain investment income (and therefore improve the bottom line), there really is not much difference between strategies when it comes to the most likely (mean) result. Even the downside (0.1 percentile) results are all about the same. In fact, staying the course gives the company a better upside opportunity than changing strategies. A rather counterintuitive result, but one that can be easily communicated to the Board with an explanatory graph using DFA.

In this example, the company is trying to determine if it should increase its allocation to equities. Notice how total return (consisting of all interest and dividend income, plus unrealized and realized gains and losses) varies significantly depending upon the level of equities. This is to be expected, since equities are quite a bit more volatile than fixed income investments.

NOTE 3-1

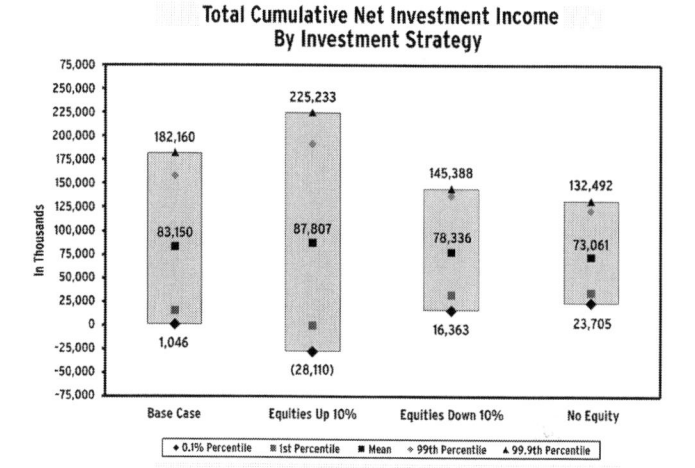

Total Cumulative Net Investment Income By Investment Strategy

	Base Case	Equities Up 10%	Equities Down 10%	No Equity
99.9th Percentile	182,160	225,233	145,388	132,492
Mean	83,150	87,807	78,336	73,061
0.1% Percentile	1,046	(28,110)	16,363	23,705

Legend: ♦ 0.1% Percentile ▪ 1st Percentile ■ Mean ◊ 99th Percentile ▲ 99.9th Percentile

However, this exhibit comes with an interesting story of its own. This analysis was put together when one of the most influential members of a Board (you know, the one with the loudest baritone) suggested that increasing equity levels was the best strategy. When this Board member saw the graph, he asked, 'Does this mean that in the worst case (0.1 percentile), if we increase equities all of our investment income would be more than wiped out by realized and unrealized losses?' When we told him, 'yes it does,' he quickly stated, 'well, there is no way we should increase equities!'

DFA requires quite a bit of work, but when it is done correctly it can provide some very interesting insights as well as assist senior management and the Board in making decisions aligned with their risk appetite.

NOTE 3-2

Sure Bob is pointing out the obvious here, but let's move this into reality. Many, many companies do not have a very good idea of the duration of their liabilities. Generally speaking, duration is the weighted average time period of the present value of cash flows. It is a concept that can be applied to any stream of cash, income, expenses, benefits, etc. However, for insurance company reserves it can be difficult to estimate the amount and timing of future benefits that are all included in the company's reserves (liabilities).

In practice, life insurance companies have an easier time of this than property/casualty companies. Life insurers can use the 'law of large numbers' to estimate the most likely amount and timing of cash flows. This is done by estimating things like mortality, surrender rates, etc.

However, for some property/casualty companies the thought of a duration of liabilities is practically an anathema. They would ask, "How can our reserves have a duration when cash flows are based upon events that are not easily estimated—especially for lines of business with 'long tails' (i.e. long periods of time until all of a claim's benefits are paid)?" Or they may say, "We are 'cash-flow positive' (premiums nearly always exceed claims), so why should it matter what the duration of our reserves are, since they are always growing?"

NOTE 3-2

The first objection to the calculation of the reserves' duration should be met with the obvious. We must estimate what we need to have in reserves in order to fairly represent the financial position of the company; and that estimation requires an idea of the amount and timing of those benefits. From there duration can be calculated.

The second objection of being 'cash-flow positive' is a bit more difficult to overcome. But, it really comes down to how one views insurer reserves. The amount shown on the balance sheet does indeed have an estimation of the amount and timing of claims paid. The fact that the insurer is generating premiums in excess of current benefits paid merely means that it will have greater investment flexibility than if the opposite was true. However, that fact does not obviate the imbedded cash flows in the insurer's reserve amount.

Nonetheless, over the years, we have seen an increasing embrace of the idea of duration of liabilities (reserves) by both property/casualty and life/health insurance companies. And determining duration of liabilities is a key component in understanding how those funds should be invested.

NOTE 3-3

Although Bob appears to be a pretty easy grader, his basic approach makes sense. We noted earlier that DFA captures all sorts of asset, liability, premium, expense and other cash flows. And, then tries to determine how the insurer's financials will look when the impacts of those flows are combined. A good DFA process will be one that is easy for senior management and the Board of Directors to understand; and it should become a key decision-making tool for the company.

Of course, DFA is never there to provide a 'final answer', but should be used as any other financial tool—a guide to better understanding of the financials and, with that, improved decision making.

NOTE 3-4

Once the insurer has a good handle on its overall risk/reward, as indicated by a DFA or ALM analysis, the next step is going a bit deeper into asset allocation strategies.

ALM or DFA can help us determine key preferred risk parameters for the company like duration, credit risk, etc. And, it can be used to determine how big a 'risky bucket' we should have—assets invested for long-term growth, usually a percentage of surplus. However, ALM or DFA do not help one determine what should be in that risky bucket. For that, we should utilize the traditional efficient frontier analysis noted by Bob. We call this approach Surplus Optimization.

In this approach, we look at assets that are not core fixed income and that fit within the risk appetite of the insurance company. In the example below, the company wanted to know what mix of various equity indices would produce the most 'efficient' result (highest reward for least amount of risk). The analysis combines these indices in various mixes to develop an 'efficient frontier' of combinations that produce that relationship.

In this example, the company's existing mix is shown as 'XYZ' and it is well below the efficient frontier. That means there are other asset mixes that would produce a superior risk/reward tradeoff. On the efficient frontier, we have highlighted the minimum risk point. In addition, we have highlighted points on the curve that produce superior asset mixes with the same risk or the same reward as the company's current surplus portfolio.

NOTE 3-4

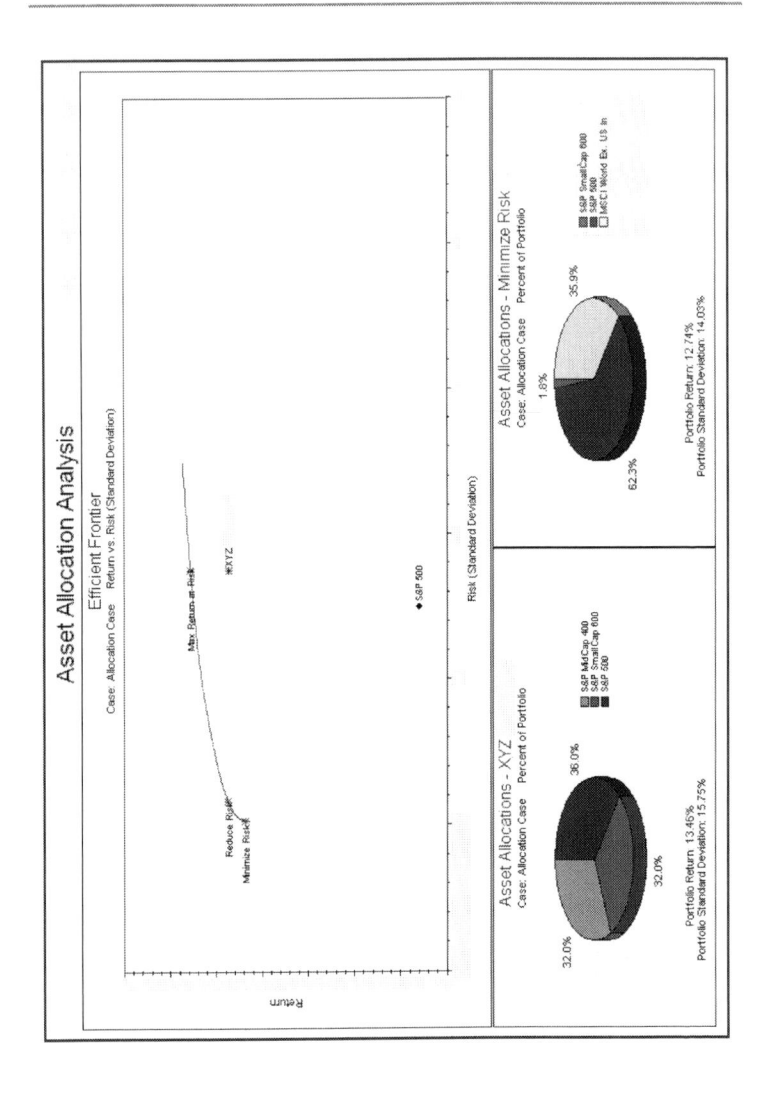

NOTE 3-4

In reality, the company did not want to take on additional risk, so it gravitated to the minimize risk portfolio on the efficient frontier. The result is shown in the pie graphs. The minimize risk portfolio reduced investment in small cap and mid cap, while increasing investment in the broader S&P 500 and adding a new investment in foreign securities.

Obviously, the Surplus Optimization analysis, like any efficient frontier approach, is highly dependent upon the assumptions of risk (usually standard deviation), reward (total return) and correlation amongst the asset classes. Thus, stress testing, something discussed later, will be very important in understanding how those assumptions might have biased the results.

NOTE 3-5

Effectively using DFA, Surplus Optimization, or any other financial modeling tool is all about giving all interested and effected parties a stake in the model. The CIO should never put this together on his or her own. That would be inviting disaster. The key is that everyone on the senior management team must have some level of 'ownership' in the process. And, it is even better if the Board feels that same sense of 'ownership'.

Thus, the use of a formal or informal committee involving investment, actuarial and marketing areas of the company will be crucial to the success of setting investment strategy. And this committee must apply its own risk appetite to the results. We will discuss this further in the next chapter. But the question around risk appetite comes down to how risk/reward is balanced and is it to the liking of the committee? As we noted, reward should be a metric tied to the company's key performance indicators of success. So, for example, the reward might be net income, net investment income, total return, return on surplus or other measures. And, the risk should be some measure of variability of that reward like standard deviation, downside deviation, probability of failing to meet a minimum risk capital benchmark or other measure.

The most successful implementations of DFA or ALM certainly have this cooperation between traditional silos as a key characteristic. And they also use understandable analytics to quantify risk and reward, in

NOTE 3-5

order for committee members to apply their own risk appetite to the decision.

Finally, once senior management has a good handle on their preferred strategic asset allocation, it is vital that the Board of Directors fully understand the basic assumptions, how the analyses were performed, and how to interpret the output that led to senior management's decision. For, ultimately, it is the Board, applying its own risk appetite, that must approve the general outlines of an investment strategy that are then embodied in the investment policy.

4

STEERING THE INVESTMENT PORTFOLIO TO SUCCESS

Bob stood beside his laptop, looking down at the PowerPoint slide on the screen for guidance. He failed to find it, wishing for the umpteenth time that the Return key were larger. Fumbling to find it distracted him, making him lose his place, or worse, his train of thought. Anxiety does that, he told himself. Set it aside! Set it aside! A busted career was not a war. Concentrate on the here and now!

"I call this section 'Steering the investment portfolio—to success,'" he told his audience, sounding for the moment less than successful. "The key consideration in developing an investment policy for an insurance company is that you *must* make sure it's tied to the company's strategic asset allocation. The next thing you have to consider—and this is paramount!—is the risk appetite of the company's board and its senior managers."

Bob paused, making a mental note to add a page that would flash just two words: 'Risk Appetite.' The phrase was too good to choke down with nerves. White letters on a red background, perhaps, with a wrap like the ones you saw around expressions like *Zap*, *Wham* and *Crunch* in comic strips. [SEE NOTE 4-1]

Bob reined himself in, focusing fast. "Right. Moving along!" he announced. This was not a good day. He opened his mouth, remembering to look towards his audience, not his notes.

"Um, in the investment policy you write for your company, never forget that you are putting pen to paper on a document that will be followed, discussed, reviewed and much of it put into effect by investment managers; and studied to death by auditors, rating agencies, regulators, and all manner of vested interests, so you have to be very careful what you put into it. Here's my advice. Be very explicit as to what an insurance company may invest in, and what it will not be investing in over my dead body—or yours! Oh, shut up, Molly. Hold it in, for Pete's sake. Sit!"

Bob threw a Kibble to the shih-tzu pacing back and forth across the French doors, staring soulfully up at the handles. Now she sat, staring just as soulfully at Bob, all coal-black eyes in a fluffy white mop of face. "O.K., I admit that wasn't a stellar performance, but I gotta tell you, Molly, you're a major distraction and a lousy audience!" Bob reached into his pocket for another dog biscuit before deciding it might be the wrong thing to do. "I guess I should have said 'Sit!' before we started."

Hmm, Bob told himself as he fetched Molly's leash, we could have had a catastrophic failure of communication!

Susan had taken the baby, Sarah, to the market, leaving Bob with Molly. He opened the door, locked it behind them, and Molly happily led her master along the side of the house and down the street.

The day was fine, traffic was light, and Molly pulled ahead, charting a familiar course. She was twelve years old with a touch of arthritis in her front right leg, but she could still pull. Bob had lost most of his anger and some of his anxiety but this whole misadventure had seriously unsettled him. Anxiety displaced short-term memory in his experience, making it hard to concentrate unless one was rooted in the Now.

"So how was my presentation?" he asked the dog. "Was it all right for you?" Out in the air he felt more relaxed. So did Molly, it seemed. She wagged her stump of a tail.

"Here's the crux of the challenge, Molly. I listed all sorts of people—or categories of people—back in the house. To get their total buy-in you and they have to be moving in lockstep. Here's the winning formula: A good investment manager plus a well-reasoned strategic asset allocation plan requires a third factor—open, well-trafficked lines of communication to and from everyone concerned. Up, down and sideways. Then, and only then, do you get total buy-in. Then, and only then, do you excel at your job.

"Then, and only then," he added, "can you defend your ass!"

They had taken a few more steps before Bob went on, "Molly, I've understood and practised all those things for years. I thought I did them well, but I never expressed that total synergy in one seamless equation."

The dog trotted along unmoved, turned a corner and entered nirvana. A small wood interrupted the flow of houses, coming right to the edge of the sidewalk. The township had added a hydrant here anticipating houses that had never been built. It seemed to have just one purpose, as a magnet for dogs.

"Where are you going, Molly? Which one today?" For the moment, variety of choice overwhelmed the shih-tzu. "Were you aware, Molly, that the world only knows about the philosophy of Socrates because Plato turned him into a character and debated him in his *Dialogues*? I could enshrine you in my *Presentations* as a character, *Canis domesticus Moll*, but first you have to *respond*!"

Molly had more important things on her mind. She whined and tugged at her leash. Bob bent to release her and she shot into the bushes, leaving her master playing Plato by himself.

"That's often the problem. Too much choice. Unless you train yourself to be disciplined, that can be a real trap." Bob whirled Molly's leash conspicuously. Talking to a dog was one thing; talking to oneself, another. "On the risk appetite side," Bob projected his voice, "we have to make sure folks understand that risk appetites *do* change. It's one thing to consider risk appetites as theoretical models and long-term personal relationships with vendors you're reluctant to break. But it's then that a risk can hit you 'upside the head.' Suddenly we see it differently." [SEE NOTE 4-2]

Not for the first time Bob understood why so many single people own dogs. It's acceptable, even obligatory, for dog owners to talk to each other when their pets meet in the park. Having a dog extends the range of acceptable human behavior—including that of communication.

In the blink of an eye Molly shot under a bush, flushing out a squirrel that took off across the road. A driver honked, braked, swerved and drove on. No damage done, but Bob looked after the car as if he were conducting an experiment, observing that the driver didn't immediately speed up again. Funny, that. Humans, or their circumstances, can change and they suddenly look at risk differently. After an accident, he told himself, people inevitably drive more carefully than they did before. The same things happen in financial markets. Risk appetites change, and they can change fast.

"Come on, Molly, let's get back to our presentation. Here, girl." Molly returned to heel obediently and Bob hitched her to the leash. "Here's your last lesson today." He slipped Molly a biscuit. "When you're setting out an asset allocation, you must try to anticipate what might happen to your client's tolerance for risk. It can go up; it can go down. Sometimes a change has something to do with the business and it makes good sense. Other times—like in a real downturn—people totally over-react.

Whoa," Bob had to haul back on her leash as they approached the house. "You have to advise moderation in that respect."

Bob fed Molly, mopped up slopped water around her bowl and clicked his tongue. Molly responded, following her master to the study. Bob ordered, "Lie down!" Molly stepped into her basket and went to sleep.

Bob turned off his sleeping computer and returned to the legal pad and pencil. The last thing he had drawn that morning looked like a figure of eight on its side with a short length of chain between the two circles. What had he meant? Of course. Handcuffs! Here was the start of a graphic for his presentation. He penciled a headline: The key consideration. In the left cuff he wrote: 'When developing an investment policy for an insurance company...' To the short length of chain he added: 'Tie it to...' And in the right cuff, 'The company's strategic asset allocation.'

Bob put down his pencil, admiring his handiwork. The concept worked. He had a friend who might run up a few graphics in watercolor with the calligraphy to go with it. All in good time.

Now to develop risk appetite.

He penciled the phrase, wrote it again 'RISK APPETITE,' and finally put a ring around it. How, he asked himself, might the advice of an investment officer to insurance companies differ from the advice that same person might give to a non-insurance company? *It is different*, he wrote on his pad, *because insurance companies are subject to influences specific to their industry. It's more rigorously regulated than other sectors.*

It's also different from company to company, depending on their capitalization, or—Bob's pencil hovered above his pad before he wrote—*it depends how rich they are!*

He had been working at this all morning. It was coming along better than expected. Bob put down his pencil.

"Then again, investment advice to an insurer *must* be different," he announced to the empty room before whistling softly at Molly.

The dog cocked an ear, rejected the intrusion and went back to sleep.

"Some help you are." Bob swiveled his chair to address the rest of the house. "Your approach to giving advice depends on your client company's lines of business, the risk appetite of its board, and of other stakeholders. Insurance companies have objectives, and they need advice that is unique."

Bob leaned back in his chair, linked his hands behind his head and addressed the newel-post at the foot of the stairs. That, and the bottom three steps, were all the staircase he could see. "No other industry has so many rating agencies looking over its shoulder. Not just S&P, Moody's and Fitch, but then you've got A.M. Best specifically checking insurers. Then you have state regulators and accounting firms acting as quasi-regulators when it comes to insurance firms because of their nutty pronouncements."

Bob paused to take in the silence, only to be thwarted by Molly's snoring. He swiveled towards the dog. "D'you know, Molly, you get FDIC insurance if you're a bank depositor, but policy holders don't. Each state has a guarantee association, but most people have never heard of them, never mind whether a guarantee association could cover a major call on its funds. They're private entities, in case one of their member companies goes insolvent. They work state by state, supposedly compensating for shortfalls when insurers can't keep promises they make to their policy holders. Mind you, they'd be in a mess if a single state got into major trouble.

"I don't think an insurance company can ever go bankrupt legally," he mused. "It can go into insolvency, or be rehabilitated. Lawyers tell me that insurers aren't written into the bankruptcy code. Depending on how they're set up, their parent companies can legally go bankrupt, but not insurers." The dog didn't seem to care.

Bob missed the sound of the key in the door, but Molly didn't. She was out of her basket and pawing the narrow glass pane beside the front door before Bob could get out of his chair.

"Hi, Sue," he called. "I'll take the groceries. You unwrap Sarah." They traded a quick kiss before carrying bundles back through the hall to the kitchen. "How's the market?" he asked.

"Busy. I think everyone's dodging the rain." Susan unzipped the baby's Dr. Denton and lifted her clear. "Hm, she needs changing."

"I'm not surprised. You've been gone awhile." Bob volunteered, "I'll do it."

"Feed Molly, Honey! I'll change Sarah. How's the writing going?"

"We've had a good day, Molly and I. We had a full and frank discussion covering points of mutual interest. Didn't we, Moll?" The shih-tzu was sliding around on the kitchen tiles, trying for traction to place herself under the bag of dry food in Bob's hand.

"No fooling. Seriously, Bob. How're you doing?"

"Sue, I wouldn't lie to you. It's going fine."

"I'm glad." His wife sounded relieved. "Have you finished for the day?"

"No. I still have 'Five steps of best practices investment policy' to write."

"Go do it, then. I'll bring cookies and coffee when you're done."

"Ah, the old 'Best way to a man's heart is through his stomach' trick."

"I hope I already won your heart!"

"Of course you did."

Susan smiled. "Give me a heads-up when you're ready."

Bob eyed the dog, her stump of a tail wagging, her front end buried in her bowl. "O.K., Sue, I won't be long."

Back in his study, Bob picked up his legal pad and wrote: *The 5 key components of best practices investment policy.*

He was seeking a way to summarize them as bullet points, but then he decided to spell them out first.

Bullet point 1, he wrote: *The first key component is the preamble, which sets out who takes responsibility for what; the roles and responsibilities of a company's investment committee, of its board, and of its CIO and all the other major players.* [SEE NOTE 4-3]

Bullet point 2: Assess and describe investment return objectives and management's objectives.

This, he noted, gets right into what you want to accomplish with your portfolio. Are you looking for yield, or total return? Which is the more important to your company, and to what extent? That's usually a central topic. [SEE NOTE 4-4]

Bullet point 3: Asset allocation and risk guidelines.

This is typically what people think about when they consider investment policy. They think of the limits, the parameters. They have to live with the proportions they've set for each asset class: so much per security, per issuer, so much in this, so much in that, no more than X% in a given credit rating. A portfolio with a duration of Y may not contain more than Z% in equity investments, or in other types of investments.

Bob paused, shoved his pencil into a sharpener and cranked it. Then he wrote, underlining: *Too many people think of those guidelines as a limit when they come to defining policy, but policy is more than that!!!* [SEE NOTE 4-5]

Bob could smell coffee brewing and hear Susan fussing over Sarah. He felt exiled in his study by his yellow legal pad—but he was also firing on all cylinders with a clear view of what he had to say:

Bullet point 4: Investment performance and reporting. Here's where the investment policy you write specifically outlines key performance benchmarks. What benchmarks are we using? He paused, then began to scribble faster—*we'll get into customized benchmarks later. And* customized *versus* peers. *We'll get into that later, too.*

Molly appeared beside his desk. Bob gave her the benefit of his wisdom: "We've seen some investment policies stipulate a return of X% above inflation, haven't we, Molly?" He bent to scratch between her ears. "Silly, that, but there's no accounting for…" The word 'accounting' caught his eye. Bob drew a ring around it. [SEE NOTE 4-6]

Now comes the reporting part for bullet point 4, he wrote. Who's responsible for reporting what? What sort of reports will the investment committee and the board receive?

Next comes bullet point 5: We need to talk about investment policy and the evaluation of guidelines. A marksman is only as good as the foresight on his gun. Bob paused to underline this impromptu simile. He was nearly finished.

Bullet point 5 may be the most important section of investment policy, he wrote. What's important here? This is where we say: We have to review this, X times a year. Who do we make personally responsible for that?

Bob drew the outline of an hourglass-shaped timer, followed by a rough note that read: *Typically this gets an annual complete review.* [SEE NOTE 4-7]

Bob put down his pencil and closed his eyes, weary. He had reached a logical point to break off. Or had he? Over the years Bob had discovered that he could glean information, hints, even useful chunks of research by picking up a source, any source, at random, flipping its pages and reading what lay there in black and white. The power of suggestion—or, rather, the power to discover valid suggestion in seemingly unrelated sources—was indeed a valuable trait. Mark Twain had written about it. Bob reached across his desk, picked up his tattered Xenophon, riffled its pages and stumbled into Book 6,

Section 5. He read:

"Sirs, we must see if the offerings favor us, if the omens are propitious, if the victims' entrails look promising."

Of course! The entrails! How could he have overlooked the obvious next point? He picked up his pencil and wrote:

How do you stress-test an investment policy?

Once more he glanced at the book:

"The officers bade him lead on. Nobody argued, and he led the way."

Bob smiled, dropping the book on his desk. Advising on investment policy was, once again, a matter of leadership in action and of dynamic leadership during action, of knowing what to ask, when to ask, and taking charge.

Just yesterday he had been not so much surfing as churning the Internet for inspiration when he stumbled on a sentence he right away scribbled on a Post-it note. Now he transcribed that axiom to his notepad: *'High performers recognize shifts in the landscape before they happen.'* He added:

Q: What level of detail do we go into here?

A: We take the given limit we already set in the investment plan and ask: What happens in the worst case if we run up to that limit? If we have a 20% limit on Triple-B bonds, what's the stress test, what are the worst case losses we might take, and are we comfortable with that? [SEE NOTE 4-8]

Then,—*How do you quantify risk measurement within your investment policy?*

The first thing is—Bob was on a roll—*you have to remember that your investment policy is tied to your strategic asset allocation, which is tied to your overall risk management process. Three points welded together by chains. Keep the whole program in lockstep.* He added a few mischievous words, from Xenophon's battle orders: *"Slow march and even pace. No one to quicken into a run."*

Bob closed his eyes before starting to write again: *That takes* us back—no matter the state of the market—to the investment discipline of Asset Liability Management (ALM), and/or dynamic financial analysis (DFA). The profession of investing demands the mental discipline of war!

Then, as if to explain his previous sentence, he added another few words he had glimpsed: *"So they formed in compact line and advanced."*

"Bob, shall I make the coffee?" Susan stood in the door.

"I'm almost there, Sue. Ten minutes should do it."

"O.K." She disappeared back into the hall.

Bob was steaming along now. The thing about writing, he had discovered, is that if you keep doing it past a certain threshold of exhaustion it gets easier, not harder. A tired mind stops imposing resistance.

There are other, ongoing measures within the protocols of an investment policy that we use to quantify risk measurement, he wrote. *One of those is a policy's duration. That's the risk that the interest rate will change. The other thing is the convexity, and that's a whole other story. It's complicated.*

He looked across the table at the Anabasis, ragged as an old phone book. He had studied passages from this, from Sun Tzu's *The Art of War*, and from other greats in his West Point days. Now he recalled: "In difficulties he did not lose his head, as all who ever served in a campaign with him would with one consent allow." That had been a guide to his career in war and peace. And what had happened to derail that career? He was still trying to make sense of that. Once he succeeded on that front, he reasoned, there would be no more outbursts of anger.

Bob made his final note for the day: *The other thing is the convexity. That's complicated. Convexity is duration changing with interest rate. Expand this!* he jotted down. *Too tired but I can't leave it here!* [SEE NOTE 4-9]

And, last but not least: *What credit losses will we take in our portfolio, and what do we expect? Yes, Dear People,*

UNCERTAIN TIMES | 63

he wrote. *We can't have negative returns and not take losses. People are realizing, when we buy corporate bonds, we do not necessarily receive that yield. The times, they are a-changing.*
[SEE NOTE 4-10]

At last Bob dropped his pencil on his yellow pad. "Sue!" he called. "Lay out the cookies, Hon."

4
CHAPTER NOTES

Hidden dangers can be inadvertent and they may be lurking in the investment policy...

NOTE 4-1

Perhaps the most difficult, yet most important, concept for any insurer to define is its risk appetite. Yet, understanding the insurer's risk appetite must be embedded in nearly every decision throughout the investment process.

Some of the possible ways to quantify Risk Appetite might be:
1. Probability of not achieving a given goal such as investment income, net income or return on surplus;
2. Probability of not achieving a desired minimum risk capital or other measure. For example, most every insurer realizes that having a BCAR (Best Capital Adequacy Ratio) greater than a given number is a necessary, though not sufficient, condition for a given targeted rating from A.M. Best;
3. A portfolio with a minimum average credit rating of 'x';
4. A portfolio with a duration within a given range;
5. Below investment grade bonds not to exceed x% of the portfolio.

NOTE 4-1

And the list of possible ways to define risk appetite can go on and on. However an insurer attempts to quantify or define risk appetite, it must be part of an exercise where both senior management and the Board are in agreement. And, most importantly, it must be something that is routinely discussed with the Board.

Too often, insurer Boards do not have the level of expertise to fully understand the business in detail. And yet, they have to make important, global decisions that can mean the difference between success and failure, or, more likely, excellent to horrible financial performance.

It is the communication of risk and all its attendant parts in a manner that the Board, as well as senior management, can fully understand that is a linchpin to a successful investment process.

NOTE 4-2

Molly might have trouble understanding the concept, but apparently so do we humans. We have this tendency to a few basic failings when it comes to understanding risk. One of those is a tendency to anchor our expectations on what has just occurred or simply to be more influenced by that which is more recent than longer-term relationships.

One is amazed when listening to what passes for explanations from the financial press when the stock market goes up, "More buyers than sellers today" or vice versa. Of course, this is impossible as every transaction must have a buyer and a seller. Yet, all too often, we go about our day taking in this information as reasonable and 'sage thoughts' from those we trust.

The same can be said for risk. How many risk managers were surprised when their models showed unexpected losses in sub prime mortgage pools? Weren't residential housing prices only supposed to go up?

NOTE 4-2

Couldn't we trust the rating agencies' assessment of the imbedded credit risk? Once again, influenced by the most recent set of events instead of the probability that things might change in a woeful manner, risk managers and investors at the largest, most trusted banks, brokers, pension funds and, yes, even insurance companies were completely fooled by these 'hidden' risks—that were not hidden at all. They spelled problems lurking in plain sight.

Conversely, with the 'Greatest Deleveraging in the History of the World' at work, and portfolios bleeding red ink, it was all too easy for Boards and senior management to 'shut the barn door after the horses bolted' and become extra cautionary. Once again, centering on the most recent events, opportunities can be missed. The key is a level head and an understanding that the most interesting events are those at the 'tails' of the probability distribution of events—and thinking through if and how your company would or should react today.

NOTE 4-3

This is perhaps the most obvious, yet the most easily ignored part of the investment policy. We have seen policies written like a detailed legal document, policies written on less than one sheet of paper and everything in between. But, it is the first key component of a 'best practices' investment policy that many insurers seem to leave in a summarized state, if at all.

Assigning roles and responsibilities and tying them to the company's overall corporate governance does more than set up an audit trail of who is supposed to do what and why. It helps set the tone for the investment process and seems to add a higher level of due diligence to the activities of those named in the policy.

NOTE 4-4

To say that the yield versus total return is a 'central topic' understates its importance. It is critical in setting the direction for the investment process.

Most every policy talks about 'mom and apple pie' issues like maintaining adequate liquidity, diversification, controlling risk and protecting investment principal. However, it is the discussion of yield versus total return that influences issues such as asset allocation, benchmarking, manager selection and style, portfolio monitoring and performance measurement. In other words, the insurer's senior management and the Board must be in full agreement on the relative importance of yield versus total return, or much misunderstanding will ensue—and that's an understatement.

Also, it is important to realize that the objectives noted in this second major section of a 'best practices' policy probably conflict with each other to some degree. For example, if you want excellent liquidity, you will buy 100% US Treasury Bills, but this is a terrible strategy if you want to achieve solid risk adjusted return or yield, etc. Thus, once again, it is important that the Board and senior management understand these conflicts and their implications, while also agreeing on their importance.

NOTE 4-5

And, as you can tell from Bob's thoughts, this section is only part of an overall 'best practices' policy. Time after time, we have seen policies that are merely made up of a set of limits, credit rating minimum, duration range, et cetera, without considering the larger goals and objectives of the investment policy, with its implications for the investment process.

Although most companies set limits based upon how they 'feel' or look to outsiders, those limits can and should be 'stress-tested' in order to determine if they truly fit within the company's risk appetite.

NOTE 4-6

And to what extent does accounting enter into determining benchmarks or comparison with peers? It does both, explicitly, in the calculation, and implicitly in the ongoing influence of the geography of financial statements (what gets put into the income statement versus the balance sheet and where), as well as the latest accounting rulings (e.g. what is 'fair value' anyway, and how does it impact Other Than Temporary Impairment?) on the overall investment process.

NOTE 4-7

As Bob has noted, consistent, annual review of the policy—or sooner should circumstances change (e.g. material merger or acquisition)—is vital to maintaining the policy as a 'living document', responsive to the risk appetite of senior management and the Board; and relevant to the overall investment process.

NOTE 4-8

The rating agencies have published studies on expected incidence and severity of loss from any given credit rating. Although we would not recommend its use for non-corporate bonds, such as sub prime mortgage backed securities, statistics for corporate bonds do have quite a depth to them.

With the usual caveats, one can use the information on defaults and recoveries given default to determine how a portfolio of any mix of rated corporates might be impacted by losses—both on an expected and a stressed basis.

NOTE 4-9

Convexity is important when reviewing assets or liabilities that are subject to imbedded options. For most insurers that would typically mean mortgage-backed securities (the imbedded option is that provided to the homeowner who can prepay their mortgage at any time) or, for life insurers, annuities that can be surrendered ('prepaid') for cash at any time.

Convexity makes the change in price of an asset move more or less than expected from just using duration as a guide. For example, a mortgage-backed security (MBS) with a duration of four years would be expected, except for convexity, to rise in value 4% for every 1% drop in interest rates (across the entire yield curve). However, a MBS typically has a negative convexity, which means you won't get the entire 4% rise. This is because that 1% drop in interest rates will probably cause some homeowners to make the call to their local bank/broker and refinance the mortgage within that MBS. Thus, with negative convexity, the investor will get back cash (prepayments) just when they don't really want it—when rates are lower. And, the result is a slight drag on that expected 4% rise in value.

And, if rates rise 1% instead of falling, that expected 4% drop in value will also be worse due to negative convexity. Why? Because as rates rise, there is less of a probability that we will see prepayments. (Why would the homeowner refinance at a higher interest rate?) That slowing prepayment 'speed' tends to actually lengthen the duration

NOTE 4-9

of the MBS. In other words, just when we want the cash to invest at a higher rate, it is tied up inside the MBS. This slight expected delay in receiving payments will mean a greater drop than the expected 4% in the value of the MBS.

NOTE 4-10

And because of the increasingly complex state of financial markets, the world economy and the insurance company, we must stay ahead of those changes as much as possible. Yes, it helps to stress-test limits, but, once again, this is a first step in understanding the risk imbedded in the policy.

Carefully thinking through as many potential pitfalls ahead of time and determining how they might be handled in the policy is vital. All too often we have seen an external manager saying they were 'within the policy' when, in reality, the policy never contemplated the strategy they executed—a strategy that might be at odds with the company's risk appetite.

Hidden dangers can be inadvertent and they may be lurking in the investment policy.

5

MIRROR, MIRROR ON THE WALL

PEER GROUP ANALYSIS:
Am I Comparing Myself to the Best or the Worst?

Bob reached his classroom early. He wasn't nervous. And it wasn't the faded primrose-painted walls that attracted him, or the array of desks that made his little group seem embarrassingly small, or the fiber panels and fluorescent tubes above.

No, he wanted time in the empty room to work out what personality he should project: Friendly? Judgmental? Cold? Military? About this, and other things, he was still uncertain. His topic for the evening, "Peer group analysis," suggested he might want to work at being a peer. He had used the term in business for a long time, but it still sounded ambiguous. It needed to be placed in context. Did it suggest judges qualified to criticize or approve portfolios? Did it mean comparable portfolios, or a group of matching entities? A loose definition included all the above. The term took in a wide range of meanings. How to explain it?

As a chief investment officer himself, Bob had noticed that

CIOs tended to be focused on their jobs. Their knowledge-base was vast, but tightly focused, and their range of human contacts, well… Freelance investment consultants had to build and maintain broader networks than employees did. Freelancers needed to make and keep clients.

So did Bob. At least for now. Maybe he should practice his neglected networking skills on his students. He had yet to perfect his "elevator speech." He sighed. He had never quite broken loose from being an Army officer, of knowing very clearly when to give orders, and who to take them from. Who was the best model in this class? Who should he play to? He looked at his list:

Sally Prentice, a former realtor turned personal finance consultant. A single mom with a five-year old daughter. So far, Sally had been pleasant, well-informed, but reserved. Had she succeeded in personal finance?

Ken Stiller. Out of a good school and into a good job as a civil servant. He was evidently bored. He was also too self-aware. Bony. Favored a corduroy suit. (He had worn one at their one and only previous class.) Looked like someone who taught English. Prickly.

Bill Hanna. A lovable overweight schlep. Bob suspected that Bill had a great way with people. Must have had a good career in insurance. He looked and behaved just right for the part. Bob imagined himself calling a theatrical booking agent: Hello, Central Casting. Please send me an example of a successful insurance salesman! Bill Hanna was the very opposite of Willy Loman.

Bob turned to the board and wrote the title of the class while trying out his opening line on the empty classroom. "Peer group analysis is surprisingly simple, as well as surprisingly difficult. It depends once again on the objectives you're trying to achieve."

"Hey, Bob, I believe you, buddy, but let me get a seat!"

Bob turned to find Bill Hanna squeezing his bulk into one of the desks, dropping his coat on another. "Hi, Bill. I'm just getting set up. I must have hit Playback too soon!" They laughed. Bob stepped forward to shake hands. Here was the "peer" he needed. He could feel himself loosening up.

"Just be yourself," Sue had told him as she kissed his cheek and showed him through the door. "Just be yourself, Bob. You're a great guy. You'll be fine."

Now, as he watched Bill Hanna unzip his writing folder, he knew he would indeed be fine.

"When I was coming in you were saying, 'Surprisingly simple, surprisingly difficult.' Reminds me of something."

"What's that?"

The big man was still breathless. *"A Tale of Two Cities.* First line."

Bob shot back, "Oh, sure. 'It was the best of times, it was the worst of times.'"

"Yea, right. But it's the next bit makes more sense where the market is now. 'It was the age of wisdom, it was the age of foolishness, it was the epoch of belief...' What can a guy believe in, Bob? This is a heck of a time to invest!"

"Which takes us back to the first line. Maybe it's not the worst of times to invest. There's a smorgasbord out there. Hi there!" Bob welcomed Ken and Sally, coming in together.

The newcomers fitted themselves into desks. Bob began again. "Bill and I were talking about..." He gestured to the title of the class on the board, "...Peer group analysis. It can be simple, but you can have a lot of complications." He paused, still hung up on precise definition. "There's a simple way to compare investment performance, and that's to take the total risk and return characteristics of an insurance company's portfolio and compare that to a whole lot of unconstrained investment portfolios. That takes us back to last week. What do I mean by unconstrained?" he asked his class.

Ken Stiller replied, "We're dealing specifically with the insurance industry. That means a whole mess of auditors and regulators at state and federal levels. They'd cut us more slack if we were investing for anything other than insurance. We would be more *unconstrained*."

Ken was using 'us' and 'we,' Bob noticed. He felt his own comfort level beginning to rise. The hardest sell among these three was buying in.

"Can you compare a 'constrained' insurance-type against typical models?" Sally Prentice asked.

"Against typical *unconstrained* models?"

She nodded.

"You can buy into several different services, but be real careful what you ask them to do. Watch them! They may end up comparing yours to an unconstrained investment portfolio where managers can buy and sell with more latitude. That's why I said: It can be simple, and it can be tough."

"But asset types are asset types across the board, aren't they?" she asked. "I mean, as long as you cross-reference asset types you're comparing apples to apples."

"Yes, but in the world of insurance there's a whole range of issues that make it more constrained. It's not just externals. Things come up that relate to your business. I had a CEO tell me, 'Bob, we need a million dollars in capital gains out of this portfolio!' All you can do is say, 'O.K.' That might not be your call on the way things are, but the investments exist to support the company."

"Sounds like you're saying insurance company investment managers have to be smarter than the rest." Ken Stiller seemed to be mentally testing his mettle against the demands of the job.

"I didn't say that, Ken. But they may have to be sharper, and faster. For example, you may have to carry less baggage from the past because you're picking up another load with these constraints. Any time you introduce a constraint you make an environment tougher and the demand for return is—well, it's no less than anywhere else!"

"But if the boss is asking for money just like that…"

"Just like that, Sally. Right."

"It changes corporate behavior."

"No. It doesn't *change* behavior if that's what you're accustomed to. Corporate behavior is consistent across the insurance industry. It's just not consistent with anywhere else."

"What you're saying, Bob, is, if you want to jump into investing for insurance companies, you'd better get used to culture shock."

"If you're new to it, Bill, I'd agree: Shock may be accurate when you start out. But, look, we get used to our working conditions. My task is to brief you for that mission."

Mission! The military term had crept in unannounced, as if he were plotting an advance across tough terrain. Bob changed his tack. "You can compare constrained to unconstrained, but you have to select your tools well. You can compare portfolios numerically; you can do style analysis, you can do charts. But that's not useful for a lot of companies because it doesn't compare them to companies in similar situations.

"Fortunately," he went on, "every insurance company in the U.S. files a statutory financial statement, so you can get a lot of detail on their investments, right down to what securities they own. You can try to do a total return on whatever insurance company has filed an annual statement."

"Sounds too good to be true." Bill looked like a kid in grade school, taking notes with his fist wrapped around his pen and his tongue between his lips.

"Well, it *is* too good."

"Uh-oh, here's the other shoe about to drop." Ken Stiller was wearing a tweed jacket and jeans tonight, looking like he'd just stepped out of an English faculty.

"That's true, Ken. You get plenty of stuff: book yields, credit ratings, things like that. But there's never enough in the statutory filings to reconstruct… D'you have a question, Sally?"

"Can you get enough information out of those filings to compare your total return to another insurance company?"

"Good question. The answer is no. There's just not enough data in those statutory filings to do an accurate comparison on returns. What you *can* compare is the general risk profile: Do you have more below-investment grade bonds than the other guy? Can you compare book yields? That can deceive you because…" Bob raised an arm to command attention. "Why? Why can good figures deceive you? Can anyone help me here?"

Sally shot back: "You can't make a direct comparison because it depends where interest rates were when two managers in two different companies bought into the investment."

"Good. My boss called me out once because he noticed a competing insurer getting much higher interest on something than we were. They'd bought in three years earlier when yields were way up. I wasn't even working for the company at the time."

Bob paused before driving home the point. "Even if it was the same investment, the other guy might have bought it months, and percentage points, apart. Of course you're getting clues across the board in real time on a real allocation mix: equities, fixed incomes… Credit rating is in there."

"So you get to connect the dots."

"Uh, right, Bill, you get to connect *some* dots…"

"I was a juror a couple of times. The more facts you get, the easier it is to link the dots and paint the picture."

"And you have to hope it's accurate, Bill. That's pretty much what I was going to say: the more experience you have, the fewer dots you need to make the links. For example, you can even *estimate* duration. I'm putting the word 'estimate' in quotes here because those statutory filings don't ask for duration. They list *maturity*."

Ken interrupted, "Meaning, 'the dog that didn't bark' still supplies a clue."

"Absolutely. There are several ways you can try to reach a reasonable conclusion."

The students were making copious notes. Bob paused to let them catch up. He caught Sally looking at her watch and remembered she had a five-year-old daughter. Where was the kid, Bob wondered? At soccer camp or ballet class? When did Sally need to pick her up?

"O.K.," he went on. "You can do all sorts of peer group type analysis. Ultimately it has to go back to that central point, about the sole purpose of investments being to support the insurance business. What you want to see is how your peers in other companies developed income from investments that then flowed to their bottom lines. Then you compare those bottom lines!"

Bob paused again to let them write. Pens were busy. He had said something worthwhile.

"Next thing, how did they reach their bottom lines? You compare net income, return on assets, return on equity, and how did the underwriting work for or against them?" Bob paused. "So you look at the overall company using the statutory statement as well as the individual investment detail." [SEE NOTE 5-1]

Pens scratched to a halt. "Let's take five minutes," Bob suggested. "I imagine you could use a break."

Sally Prentice took out her Blackberry and walked to the back of the room. Bill Hanna started drawing cartoon faces around his notes. Ken Stiller, it seemed, wasn't ready to stop. He asked, "How many companies would you model to get a useful analysis of the field?"

"If you're a consultant, that's up to the client. A lot of times they say: 'Compare me to my competitors.' But if you're a small company you're competing with multinationals as well as other small and medium sized companies."

"Is that a problem?"

"It can be. The client says: 'Compare me to Allstate.' Well, a large company typically has more investment flexibility, so it's not a fair comparison. Then, the large company is more than likely writing insurance outside your line of business. So you get apples and oranges at both ends. You're better off finding similar-size companies in similar lines of business, even if they're half way across the country."

"Yea, but writing auto insurance in Manhattan is not the same as writing it in Cedar Bluffs, Nebraska."

"Maybe it is. The dollar amounts are way different, but competitive forces constrain both markets. You're scaling up and down, but you'd be getting similar *factors*. That's apples and apples, and that's what you need."

Sally Prentice had returned to the group, and Bill Hanna had stopped doodling to listen in. Bob decided to go on.

"Remember, folks, the peers we pick for comparison may be closest in size and business. But maybe they *stink*! Bill, you got a question?"

"Yea, I get the point: Are we comparing ourselves to the '62 Mets, or the '27 Yankees?"

Ken chimed in, "The Yanks were even better in 1918."

"Nah, but that's when a sportswriter coined the term 'Murderers' Row' for them!"

The three men turned to Sally, visibly surprised. She laughed, wagging her pen. "What's the matter, guys? You think girls don't know baseball? The 1918 Yankees team was good, and that's when the fans first used that term, but where it stuck was the Babe Ruth-Lou Gehrig team of 1927!"

Bob retreated to his teacher's desk, "I can't top that, Sally, but I'll do my best. Here's another issue: the *range of results*. For example, if market yields of our portfolios both yield 5.5%, and our book yields are different, say, from 4.5 to 7.0%, then I want to know: Why? That may take some digging. It could be we already answered this question. The company we are comparing ourselves to bought the same bonds, but on different dates and therefore at different interest rates." [SEE NOTE 5-2]

This point had come up twice, Bob noted. So, answer it twice: It was clearly important. "You found a lot of that in the mid-'80s," he explained. "Stagflation sent interest rates over 20% and yields up to 13-14% in Jimmy Carter's last year. So once again you have to make a comparison from book yields. Even though we, personally, may be doing a great job, sometimes it's the luck of the draw. Timing is everything."

Bob tried to keep it casual, but he could feel anger rising. He had been out of the company over a month, more able to think objectively, even analytically, about his firing. The optics of his performance hadn't looked good, maybe; but his underlying performance had been sound. Standing there in his classroom he made a resolve: One day he would call Greening and try to get at the truth.

"Bob?" Could it be that Ken Stiller was sounding concerned?

"Yeah?"

"We thought we'd lost you there."

Bill Hanna exclaimed, "He's got baseball on his mind! Still thinking of Murderers' Row, Bob?"

"That was even before Babe Ruth and Lou Gehrig." In spite of herself, Sally was looking at her watch as she spoke.

"Yea, I guess I was taking a time-out." Bob crashed back to the present. It was time to bring his class to an end. "So that's peer group analysis in a nutshell. Everyone, and I mean everyone in the company, wants to know how *we* are doing against the other guys. Don't forget, 'we' means 'you' personally, because *you* are the sharp end, the one in the job. But if peer group analysis is going to work for you, you have to pick the *right* other guys to compare. [SEE NOTE 5-3]

In a flash, Bob picked up a marker and wrote "peer" on the board. Then he added "Com/" right in front and adjusted the spelling: "Com/pare."

"What's in a word?" he asked, rhetorically. "Just about

everything, here!" He put down the marker. "You got to realize you're going to have limitations in your analysis—because everyone does! You can lay your hands on a bunch of other people's numbers, but it still comes down to asking: Why? You gotta understand the *why*."

Ken Stiller asked, "Who's going to tell you why?"

"Well, companies often use external consultants. External investment managers, too. I implied earlier that corporate investment managers spend too much time in their cells. That's true. But they may consult their peers from time to time."

Bill Hanna wanted to know, "We can look at the peer results but there are going to be gaps, right? How can we fill in those gaps?"

"Good question, Bill. Let's be clear, everyone. Bill is asking about the gaps in the statutory statements he's reading. He's not talking about gap analysis."

"Right." Bill picked up, "That's what I meant. Gap analysis is when you need to fix gaps in your own operation. Peer group analysis is about trying to work around other people's."

Bob took a moment to frame his answer. "You can learn a lot from the annual statements of your peer group. But we are limited in what we get from our peers. In the case of total return databases we'd be typically looking at unconstrained portfolios, so—again—it's not really a fair comparison. In insurance we deal with so many constraints that they must influence the investment game. That's why, on the annual return side, when we use the annual statements, we don't get enough numbers to give total returns. Up to a point we are stuck with things like book yield, and credit rating."

"That's too imprecise," Ken Stiller retorted, abruptly.

Bob had already conned Ken's personality type. "Yes, it's imprecise. As imprecise as market and investment analysis can often be. In the first place, all you can do is to gain as much and as varied experience as fast as you can. That way you'll be better prepared for whatever happens. I guess that's my mission here," Bob went on. "To teach you how to do that.

"Look, if you train one hundred people to equal standards—I don't care what the subject is—you'll find folks clumping more or less into one of two types. The first group falls back on their training implicitly. They have been taught that something may happen, so they expect it to happen. They do fine as long as they confront exactly what they've been taught to expect. I call those folks 'British generals'. They march men by the tens of thousands into massed machine gun fire and hope for an outcome other than mass death."

Sally took a sharp intake of breath. Ken sat bolt upright. Bill looked up, intrigued—and Bob took another time-out to ask himself what part of his brain was launching this.

"I'm not kidding. In 1815 the 'British general' mentality marched 2,000 redcoats against a well dug-in American line at New Orleans; and they were still doing it a hundred years later, in World War I. They were well educated, those officers. Quite likely many of them had read the *Anabasis* in classical Greek. But they were too well trained to break old habits that no longer worked! Those guys had emotional IQ deficits as thick as bricks. They did what they did, and they continued to do it, because they didn't know what else to do.

"That is not—I repeat—*not* the quality you need for strategic asset allocation. You need to think strategically; you need to operate tactically; and most of all you need flexibility if you're going to win the game in spite of—or because of—the gaps and constraints we are talking about. Call it pragmatism if you like. You come at this with your education as a weapon, and your past experience as a tool, but you're going to meet unexpected situations where both together aren't enough. Maybe you confront something counter-intuitive and you have to set education and experience aside because they stand in the way as impediments! So you stir what you know into a single pot called intuition and imagination. That's the flexible resourcefulness, the sort of mental toughness, you need to develop."

Bob took a breath, wondering: Was this his resentment talking, stored rage, or a change dawning into an aggressive pursuit of a new, more positive future? Even as his lips were flapping he couldn't tell, but he managed to keep a close command on his private versus public utterances.

"Here's what I mean," he continued. "First French, then British, generals threw tens of thousands of men at entrenched machine guns behind barbed wire on Vimy Ridge in March and April, 1917. Tens of thousands died, achieving—total failure. Then came the Canadian Corps. Generals Byng and McNaughton insisted on taking time to plan, to reconnoiter, to invent aerial reconnaissance and creeping barrages as brand new tools of war. Aerial sorties dropped smoke flares on unseen German gun emplacements, so that by simply triangulating positions of smoke—McNaughton was a McGill-trained engineer—the Canadians plotted those emplacements as targets. The Canadian attack destroyed 85% of German artillery within hours, allowing the infantry to follow the first ever creeping barrage right into its primary objective on Vimy Ridge before noon the first day."

The silence ran for seconds.

"You can succeed in difficult missions, in difficult times, when the lie of the land and the odds are against you. But you have to plot and plan. And maybe invent. Know the terrain, discover every tool and asset you can use to grow your portfolio. There will always be gaps. You may never fill gaps, but be sure you know what and where they are. And make sure you plug good and bad examples into your memory and never forget. Any questions?"

"Not a one, captain!" It was odd that Bill should choose that reply. Bob had never told his students he'd been in the Army.

"O.K., then. That's peer group analysis. See you next week."

5
CHAPTER NOTES

What should a Peer Group Analysis really look like? Take a look . . .

NOTE 5-1

What should a Peer Group Analysis really look like? Take a look at this first part of a sample. Assuming we have chosen the 'correct' peers—something for future discussion in Bob's class—we should start with viewing the company's income and cash flow. Why? Because, as noted earlier, investments exist to support the business of the insurer. That means they provide income (as well as capital gains and losses) which is part of the broader income statement of the company.

Measurement Description	XYZ Insurance Group	1	2	3	4	5	6	7	8	Average	Difference
Operating Income As % of Average Net Admitted Assets 2002-2003											
Underwriting G/L	-0.43%	2.41%	1.74%	-0.29%	-10.46%	-7.75%	-2.26%	9.80%	0.62%	-0.74%	0.31%
Invest Inc	4.52%	4.16%	3.84%	3.79%	5.20%	6.15%	5.27%	2.93%	3.96%	4.42%	0.09%
Realized G/L	0.51%	0.68%	-0.22%	0.21%	0.20%	1.64%	0.82%	0.01%	0.06%	0.43%	0.07%
- Realized Gain/Loss - Via (OTTI)	-0.47%	-0.23%	0.00%	-0.30%	-1.05%	0.09%	-0.27%	-0.40%	-0.24%	-0.32%	-0.15%
Other Inc/Exp	0.09%	0.61%	0.02%	0.07%	-1.62%	-0.34%	-0.09%	1.46%	0.19%	0.05%	0.06%
NI b4 P/H Div	4.69%	7.86%	5.38%	3.79%	-6.67%	-0.30%	3.73%	14.19%	4.83%	4.17%	0.52%
P/H Div	0.00%	0.00%	-0.20%	-0.10%	-0.21%	-0.06%	-0.02%	0.00%	-0.03%	-0.07%	0.07%
EBT	4.69%	7.86%	5.17%	3.69%	-6.88%	-0.36%	3.71%	14.19%	4.80%	4.10%	0.59%
Taxes	0.88%	1.16%	1.50%	0.75%	-2.10%	-0.30%	0.65%	4.41%	0.28%	0.80%	0.07%
STAT Net Income	3.81%	6.70%	3.67%	2.94%	-4.78%	-0.05%	3.06%	9.78%	4.52%	3.29%	0.51%

NOTE 5-1

Notice that XYZ Insurance Company achieved a 3.81% net income result as a percentage of its admitted assets, a little better than the average of this group of peers, which registered 3.29%. How much did investment income contribute to that? Quite a bit, when comparing the investment income percentage versus pre-tax income (investment income provided nearly all of the 4.69% return on admitted assets). This compares to the average of the peers, where investment income actually contributed more than pre-tax income.

So, XYZ and its peers were highly dependent upon investment income during the year of this study. Of course, that is comparing to an average. If we look behind the averages, the comparisons get even more interesting.

Take a look at company #5, where investment income provided 6.15% of return on assets and, despite that, #5 struggled to register a small loss overall. Meanwhile, company #7 had just the opposite approach. Investment income provided just 2.91% of return on assets, but that didn't matter all that much, as pre-tax income provided over a 14% return on admitted assets. It is not surprising that the big difference between those companies was their underwriting results.

And, this is just one way to view the comparison. We could look in detail at Other Than Temporary Impairment (OTTI) charges to see which company took it on the chin—or, perhaps, was more conservative in its application of this incredibly arbitrary accounting construct.

Measurement Description	XYZ Insurance Group	1	2	3	4	5	6	7	8	Average	Difference
Portfolio Mix											
Cash	-0.15%	0.03%	1.11%	7.09%	22.37%	4.16%	0.12%	2.60%	3.75%	4.56%	-4.71%
Preferred Stock	2.04%	1.00%	4.12%	0.42%	0.57%	13.40%	0.14%	0.63%	2.59%	2.77%	-0.72%
Bonds	85.41%	76.38%	38.43%	78.96%	71.36%	78.97%	89.72%	76.20%	89.49%	76.10%	9.30%
Common Stock	11.91%	21.52%	56.33%	12.73%	5.51%	1.69%	9.27%	17.12%	3.16%	15.47%	-3.56%
- Unaffiliated	11.60%	11.35%	50.10%	3.61%	0.00%	0.16%	9.27%	13.64%	0.47%	11.13%	0.47%
- Affiliated	0.30%	10.17%	6.23%	9.12%	0.00%	1.53%	0.00%	3.48%	2.69%	3.72%	-3.42%
Mortgage Loans	0.43%	0.17%	0.00%	0.00%	0.05%	1.31%	0.00%	0.00%	0.61%	0.29%	0.14%
Real Estate	0.36%	0.90%	0.00%	0.83%	0.14%	0.48%	0.76%	3.44%	0.40%	0.81%	-0.45%
Inv. Inc. as % of Invested Assets	5.21%	4.70%	4.33%	4.11%	6.00%	6.67%	5.81%	3.28%	4.89%	5.00%	0.21%
Inv. Inc. as % of Earned Premium	9.25%	7.37%	10.38%	10.05%	29.03%	19.26%	14.38%	3.31%	13.65%	12.96%	-3.71%
Portfolio Size ($000)	8,697,185	37,693,160	6,364,900	21,395,791	28,092,942	24,871,452	3,527,408	11,440,177	34,973,274	19,666,477	-10,971,292
Unrealized G/L	0.75%	2.30%	4.62%	2.24%	0.23%	2.36%	1.22%	2.10%	0.79%	1.85%	-1.09%
Ratio - Common Stock / Surplus	37.12%	50.38%	128.85%	43.20%	25.61%	4.62%	37.65%	43.15%	13.09%	42.63%	-5.51%

UNCERTAIN TIMES | 93

NOTE 5-1

Another important driver of investment income would be their overall asset allocation, as shown here.

Notice that XYZ has about 9% more in bonds than the peer average and about 4% less equities and 5% less cash than the peers. Of course, the fixed income portfolio will typically provide higher yields than equities or cash. Thus, we have another factor contributing to the higher than average investment income as a percentage of assets for XYZ.

Meanwhile, our 'champion' of investment income to assets, #5, has achieved some of this result by emphasizing more preferred stocks versus peers. This would make one want to review the preferred portfolio to see if, perhaps, it harbors higher yielding, higher risk securities in order to increase investment income.

Of course, our conservative investor, #7, does not look as conservative when reviewing the asset allocation. Apparently, company #7 is foregoing some investment income from bonds by reallocating to common stocks in hope of long term capital gains.

These are just a few ways to interpret these initial results. In fact, there are many other conclusions that may be gleaned from this very first part of a Peer Group Analysis, but let's get back to Bob's class and consider other issues.

NOTE 5-2

And therein lies the problems of comparing yields. Despite this, one can glean some important information from those comparisons. Here is another part of a sample Peer Group Analysis.

Measurement Description	XYZ Insurance Group	1	2	3	4	5	6	7	8	Average	Difference
Sector Allocation - Bond Portfolio (NOTE: THESE ARE NOT ACTUAL NUMBERS, FOR ILLUSTRATION PURPOSES ONLY)												
ABS	0.00%	7.44%	35.07%	10.40%	1.92%	0.00%	0.00%	0.00%	0.00%	6.09%	-6.09%
Agency	20.39%	2.74%	15.87%	4.04%	1.41%	13.34%	50.34%	50.34%	50.34%	23.20%	-2.81%
CMBS	0.00%	2.87%	0.00%	0.00%	0.00%	0.00%	0.00%	0.00%	0.00%	0.32%	-0.32%
CMO - Agency	26.84%	1.82%	17.64%	0.00%	0.00%	0.00%	0.20%	0.20%	0.20%	5.21%	21.63%
CMO - Private	0.00%	0.78%	4.42%	0.00%	0.99%	0.00%	0.00%	0.00%	0.00%	0.69%	-0.69%
Corp	20.57%	27.90%	2.01%	43.18%	3.90%	29.90%	19.89%	19.89%	19.89%	20.79%	-0.22%
Mtge	0.94%	18.71%	1.03%	0.70%	5.70%	0.00%	1.38%	1.38%	1.38%	3.47%	-2.53%
Muni	0.00%	28.59%	19.59%	0.00%	67.56%	29.23%	27.51%	27.51%	27.51%	25.28%	-25.28%
Private	0.00%	2.16%	0.00%	0.00%	0.49%	4.51%	0.35%	0.35%	0.35%	0.91%	-0.91%
Treasury	31.26%	6.10%	4.37%	41.69%	16.27%	22.34%	0.34%	0.34%	0.34%	13.67%	17.59%
Yankee	0.00%	0.90%	0.00%	0.00%	1.77%	0.69%	0.00%	0.00%	0.00%	0.37%	-0.37%
Book Yields By Sector - Bond Portfolio (NOTE: THESE ARE NOT ACTUAL NUMBERS, FOR ILLUSTRATION PURPOSES ONLY)												
ABS	N/A	4.00%	4.83%	4.00%	11.77%	N/A	N/A	4.00%	N/A	4.76%	N/A
Agency	4.53%	4.07%	3.94%	4.20%	3.58%	3.66%	5.04%	4.20%	3.66%	4.44%	0.09%
CMBS	N/A	4.99%	N/A	N/A	N/A	N/A	N/A	N/A	N/A	4.99%	N/A
CMO - Agency	4.50%	4.91%	5.44%	N/A	7.57%	N/A	6.47%	N/A	N/A	5.07%	-0.57%
CMO - Private	N/A	4.75%	2.97%	N/A	N/A	N/A	N/A	N/A	N/A	3.24%	N/A
Corp	6.56%	6.94%	4.20%	4.05%	6.63%	5.26%	6.13%	4.05%	5.26%	5.84%	0.73%
Mtge	6.89%	6.24%	6.35%	4.82%	6.38%	N/A	5.37%	4.82%	N/A	6.23%	0.66%
Muni	N/A	4.60%	4.51%	N/A	4.27%	4.90%	5.18%	N/A	4.90%	4.75%	N/A
Private	N/A	7.67%	N/A	N/A	4.48%	5.46%	5.50%	N/A	5.46%	5.95%	N/A
Treasury	5.91%	4.32%	3.18%	3.00%	4.01%	4.70%	5.95%	3.00%	4.70%	4.67%	1.24%
Yankee	N/A	7.50%	N/A	N/A	8.61%	4.52%	N/A	N/A	4.52%	6.29%	N/A
Total	5.39%	5.59%	4.58%	3.62%	4.69%	4.82%	5.31%	3.62%	4.82%	4.97%	0.42%

NOTE 5-2

Notice that XYZ's book yield (bottom row in the table) is 42 basis points (0.42%) better than the peer average. But, before we laud XYZ for investing at the right part of the cycle, etc, let's ask why. Apparently, it is timely investing in US Treasuries as well as the impact of Corporates that are primarily driving this advantage (Mortgage Pass-Throughs also have higher yields, but they are a very small percentage of the portfolio, per the upper portion of this table). Of course, with Corporates, credit risk is an issue. So, we will have to review the credit ratings of the portfolio to see if XYZ's Corporate yields are due to good timing of when its cash flows were invested or perhaps due to taking on more credit risk than peers. Another reason for the difference in yields may be the interest rate risk taken (duration is one measure for this) and we will review that later.

Following up on our assessment of a couple of representative peers, we find that our investment income to assets champ, #5, must be doing that primarily with its asset allocation (as noted earlier) and not its book yields. Those yields are below the average of the peer companies.

Meanwhile, as expected, #7 sports the worst yield of the peers (tied with #3) and this is not unexpected, as it has about half its fixed income portfolio invested in typically lower yielding US Agencies.

UNCERTAIN TIMES | 97

NOTE 5-2

As you can tell, it is very important to review several comparisons with peers in order to make a comparison based on facts and some reasonable assumptions. Asking the same question about an analysis a few times can actually shed new light on the comparison.

NOTE 5-3

If your first attempt at a peer analysis does not prove useful, it might be worthwhile to take a harder look at who the peers are.

But, to determine that usefulness you must ask yourself if you are able to draw reasonable conclusions from the analysis. Before Bob continues explaining this less than 100% clear analysis in his class, let's take a look at a few other ways to compare companies using annual statement data.

Return on assets analysis is only one way to determine how a company is doing. Another way is to determine how that ROA flows into the company's ROE (return on equity, or return on surplus). And that happens with the built-in financial leverage faced by virtually every insurer. The more financial leverage, the greater the risk, but the greater potential for reward.

Measurement Description	XYZ Insurance Group	1	2	3	4	5	6	7	8	Average	Difference
Components of ROE											
ROA	3.8%	6.70%	3.67%	2.94%	-4.78%	-0.05%	3.06%	9.78%	4.52%	3.29%	0.51%
Asst/C&S	3.79	2.85	2.90	4.31	5.17	3.41	4.88	3.26	5.49	3.99	-0.21
ROE	14.43%	19.12%	10.27%	12.67%	-24.74%	-0.19%	14.94%	31.89%	24.78%	11.46%	2.96%
Policyholders' Surplus	2,789,702	16,102,895	2,782,722	6,291,542	6,045,822	9,085,440	868,202	4,538,454	8,436,295	6,326,785	-3,537,083

NOTE 5-3

Thus, XYZ was able to achieve a solid 14+% return on surplus because it is leveraged nearly 4:1, about the average for these peer companies.

Meanwhile, the companies with the most leverage had their results magnified in both a good and bad way. Company #8 multiplied its solid ROA results by over five times financial leverage to report nearly a 25% return on surplus. Meanwhile, company #4 took its difficult negative return on assets plus over 5:1 leverage to provide nearly a negative 25% return on surplus.

We have estimated duration in an analysis not shown here and, as you might expect, there is really very little difference between each portfolio—similar companies writing similar lines of business should not really have much of a duration difference. However, there are differences by sector duration. And, these differences can also explain book yield differences.

A review of credit quality can pick up differences in insurer credit risk appetite. Note that XYZ has more AAA bonds and fewer A and BBB bonds. Thus, to some degree, the company has shied away from credit risk versus its peers. This, coupled with similar duration of its corporate bond portfolio tells us that, most likely, superior corporate bond yields (as noted earlier) are probably due to timing of investment cash flows. In other words, if XYZ happened to have proportionately more cash flow, versus its peers, to invest when rates and/or spread to US Treasuries were historically high, then XYZ would benefit more than its peers.

Measurement Description	XYZ Insurance Group	1	2	3	4	5	6	7	8	Average	Difference
SVO Credit Quality - Schedule D, Bonds Only (NOTE: THESE ARE NOT ACTUAL NUMBERS, FOR ILLUSTRATION PURPOSES ONLY)												
1 - Bond Highest (AAA - A)	100.00%	79.44%	100.00%	98.29%	96.62%	99.31%	94.39%	98.29%	79.44%	95.62%	4.38%
2 - Bond High (BBB)	0.00%	10.59%	0.00%	1.71%	3.03%	0.69%	5.26%	1.71%	10.59%	2.77%	-2.77%
3 - Bond Medium (BB)	0.00%	3.59%	0.00%	0.00%	0.00%	0.00%	0.34%	0.00%	3.58%	0.61%	-0.61%
4 - Bond Low (B)	0.00%	5.94%	0.00%	0.00%	0.00%	0.00%	0.00%	0.00%	5.94%	0.92%	-0.92%
5 - Bond Lower (CCC)	0.00%	0.35%	0.00%	0.00%	0.00%	0.00%	0.00%	0.00%	0.35%	0.05%	-0.05%
6 - Bond-Nr Def (D)	0.00%	0.03%	0.00%	0.00%	0.35%	0.00%	0.00%	0.00%	0.09%	0.03%	-0.03%
Estimated Credit Quality - Major Rating Agencies (Summary) (NOTE: THESE ARE NOT ACTUAL NUMBERS, FOR ILLUSTRATION PURPOSES ONLY)												
AAA	85.48%	55.59%	91.37%	57.81%	69.99%	67.97%	78.91%	57.97%	67.97%	72.44%	13.03%
AA	0.00%	12.57%	6.57%	9.59%	15.93%	18.50%	4.92%	9.59%	18.50%	9.73%	-9.73%
A	12.88%	10.80%	2.06%	30.89%	10.70%	12.81%	10.21%	30.89%	12.81%	12.91%	-0.03%
BBB	1.65%	10.86%	0.00%	1.71%	3.03%	0.73%	5.61%	1.71%	0.73%	3.37%	-1.72%
BB	0.00%	3.85%	0.00%	0.00%	0.00%	0.00%	0.34%	0.00%	0.00%	0.60%	-0.60%
B	0.00%	5.83%	0.00%	0.00%	0.00%	0.00%	0.00%	0.00%	0.00%	0.83%	-0.83%
CCC - D	0.00%	0.51%	0.00%	0.00%	0.35%	0.00%	0.00%	0.00%	0.00%	0.13%	-0.13%

NOTE 5-3

There are a few outliers in their credit risk profile within these peers, but perhaps the largest one is company #1, with nearly 10% of its fixed income portfolio below investment grade (below BBB). Unsurprisingly, company #1 has a portfolio with the highest book yield. Of course, what one eventually receives from bonds is their interest payments plus principal. The problem is that the more credit risk in a bond, the less likely that principal will be returned in full and in a timely manner.

As you can tell, a peer analysis can tell us a lot about how an insurer compares to others. But, its use should be tempered with a full knowledge of the limitations of the data from which the analysis springs.

6

TO CHOP OR TO STRETCH?

THE LITTLE MATTER OF PORTFOLIO BENCHMARKING

What is the measure of a man? What is the measure of a man? What is the measure of…

"Damn!"

"What's the matter, Bob?"

"Nothing, Sue. Just thinking."

"I know you better than that. What's hurting you?" Sue did indeed know her husband well, although they had not started out as a couple. They had been classmates in high school. By the time Bob went off to the Academy and into the Army they had forgotten each other.

Now he told her, "It's between me and my head, O.K.?"

"Please, Bob, share it. Please! Let's not go back to the other day."

"If you must know, I'm angry."

"And you're tearing yourself apart. Again! Why now?"

Bob paused before dismissively shuffling the paper on his desk. "I'm writing class notes on benchmarking. Benchmarking!

I've spent days writing this stuff and everything I put on paper mocks me as the reason those clowns fired me!"

"Oh, Honey, can't you distance yourself and move ahead?

Bob considered his wife's suggestion, marking the worry in her face. "You're right, Sue. I'll make some coffee and calm down."

"I'll make the coffee! You take a break. Go in the sitting room and watch the birds. There's lots of action at the feeder."

He took her hand, squeezing it a moment before he walked away. It wasn't his wife's fault he'd been fired. Or was it?

Bob had acquitted himself with distinction. Career prospects had been good. He was due to move on to more responsibility. That was how it had been—in the Army! But sometime around the end of his tour in Iraq, Bob decided that Army life was not for him.

Home on leave, he had bumped into Sue outside a coffee shop. He hadn't recognized her at first: it must have been seven, eight years. Their photos looked out of the same class yearbook. That was about as close as they had ever been.

But the next few minutes at that coffee shop evolved almost automatically. They found a table and he bought them some expensive sort of caffeine with froth. Looking back, that had been their first date.

Bob had wanted out of the Army for months before he met Sue. Looking forward to marrying her became a fine excuse for resigning his commission. But that had been then! Now he was out of the Army *and* a good job. And it was her fault! If he had stayed in the Army he would still be rising through a lifetime career.

In his heart of hearts Bob new perfectly well he was searching for people to blame apart from himself. His former bosses, his wife, their mortgage, the dog…

An angry *ego* twists things that way. It's the anger. It casts around for villains, setting up innocents as well as the guilty.

Of course, anger itself was the villain that still rose to the top of the mind and poisoned his thoughts.

Sue called him, "Coffee's ready!"

Bob jumped to his feet and went to the kitchen. Sue handed him a cup of fresh brew. He took it, careful of the heat, immediately setting it down before taking her in his arms. To her surprise he kissed her. "I'll feed the birds," he told her. "They'll need it after the first snow last night. *This*, and winter coming, too!"

"Don't say that, Bob."

"I'm working at trying to put some sort of Zen-like space between me and our troubles, Sue. I just didn't get there yet." Bob kissed his wife again and headed off to feed the birds.

"Bob!" Her voice was soft.

He turned to look at her. "What is it, hon?"

"Zen doesn't mean 'space.' It means closeness, banishing worries and living right Now." He was about to speak when she added, "You forgot your coffee."

Minutes later he was feeling better, back at his desk and considering birds. It was surely no coincidence that the miserable thirteenth and fourteenth centuries in Europe held a special fascination for drawn and sculpted birds. They represented a sense of freedom and escape. He took advantage of his respite from dark thoughts, grabbing his notepad and starting to write:

In the world of investments you typically develop benchmarks that are tied to total returns, or they're tied to yield on investment income. This evening I want to talk, he added, about total return benchmarks.

The central idea of a benchmark is that it should consist of whatever one can invest in without the aid of an investment manager. Base it on the entire universe of possible securities!

He read over his notes, surprised to discover that he wrote as if he were jotting down spoken dialogue. It was, he reasoned, a useful skill. He bent over his yellow pad again.

But!—and this is a big but! You have to customize your benchmark so it's similar to the style or the type of investments you would typically invest in for your company.

Here, Bob wrote expansively on his yellow pad, *I'll give you an example! If you wouldn't typically take your company into a lot of U.S. securities because of their relatively low yield, then don't stick too many of them into your benchmark.*
[SEE NOTE 6-1]

Molly snuffled into the study. Bob threw her a Kibble from the small bowl he kept on his desk.

"Good girl, Molly. Where's your basket? Go to sleep!"

Without further ado she made a beeline for her basket, kicked her blanket around, looked at Bob for approval—"Good girl, Molly. Lie down!"—and closed her eyes.

"Lord," Bob told himself, "that dog is suggestible."

He went back to his notes: *A lot of insurance companies and institutional investors benchmark their core fixed income against the Lehman Aggregate...* Bob paused. Lehman was no more! The pieces had been taken over.

He put a line through Lehman, substituting *"Barclay's Capital Aggregate Index."*

Pausing, he put his hands behind his head and leaned back in his chair. Remarkably, he felt relaxed. He registered the fact with pleasure, and with hope.

He went back to work. *Now,* he wrote, *you may find an aggregate index with 25% to 30% Treasuries. No way most insurers invest that way! If your company doesn't, you don't do it either!*

Bob considered his potential audience. To begin with he had his three actual students. After them, the world was his oyster —as an author and lecturer on strategic asset allocation, perhaps. He visualized his students, deciding he would pitch his notes as if to Bill Hanna. Bill was the most *simpatico*.

"O.K., Bill. Here goes!"

He wrote: *To get around the Barclay's Aggregate's constraints, Bill ol' buddy, in the fixed income world you develop a custom benchmark. Now, your weightings will be different for different sectors. You make up your custom benchmark from portions—sub-indices, if you like—of that Barclay's Capital Aggregate Index. So your weightings are different by sectors. You might have less in Treasuries, more in investment grade corporate bonds and/or in high-rated mortgage-backed securities, or commercial mortgage-backed securities.*

Bob noticed his spelling mistake, deciding to leave it. Heck, he was not in the Army and these were personal notes. He drew a ring around 'mortgage' and moved on.

"Your benchmark should mirror the typical type of investment the insurer would make," he announced to the sleeping Molly.

Sue's voice called from the sitting room, "Did you say something?"

"No, honey. I'm trying my lines on Molly."

"Good luck."

"I'm not getting through."

"Grab her l-e-a-s-h and go to the door."

"Not a chance. Not yet."

Bob picked up a Kibble and lobbed it towards the sleeping dog. It hit her on the shoulder. She reacted as if scratching a flea.

"Make the benchmark mirror the investment," he repeated. "That is absolutely the best way to test whether your investment manager did better than if you had taken a passive approach!"

So that, Bob wrote, *is ONE benchmark*. He started a new paragraph.

The next layer on top of that is to look at things on a risk-adjusted basis. On second thoughts, I'll get into that when we talk about performance management. He crossed the line through and wrote himself a memo:

UNCERTAIN TIMES | 109

Remind them about those sectors further up! How do you develop what those sectors are? Bob found his reference to 'different sectors' way back up the page, drew a line to it right across his text and put a circle around it.

He wrote: *Your benchmark should represent a function of that strategic asset allocation into sectors. If you think your strategic asset allocation should be 5% in Treasuries long-term, then your benchmark should be 5% of the Long Term Treasury sub-index of the Barclay Capital Aggregate Bond Index.*

"I guess we call that index the Barclay's Agg now," he told the dog. Then, "Sue!"

From the other room, "Uh-huh?"

"Come see. Our cardinals are back."

Susan came quietly into the room, standing with her back to the wall across from the window so her movement wouldn't startle the birds.

"They're both on the feeder," Bob said. "It must be the snow."

"That's unusual," she told him. "One of the pair usually sits up on a branch to keep a look-out for the other." Sue pointed at Molly. "Will you w-a-l-k this beast? Or will I?"

"I'll finish this up in an hour. Then I'll take her. I could use the break."

Sue blew a kiss, glanced at their pair of cardinals, and left.

Bob wrote: *Up in a branch... Keep a look-out. Where to go next? RISK FACTORS, that's where!*

He sighed, tapped his pencil, and began: *Where it gets complex is when you start to look at some of the risk factors.*

If you start moving those sub-indices around you may get a different duration from the one your strategic asset allocation says you ought to have. So you have to balance it again, till your custom benchmark resembles what your saa says it oughta be.

He must be getting tired. Bob usually wrote things out, even familiar phrases. Hey, let 'saa' stand! It was starting to get dark.

He wrote a single word, *Greening*, following that with a quote: "If I could only write, I'd write a letter to the mayor, if he could only read" Great line! Right on! Bob didn't have to look for the source. He'd been cleaning out an uncle's effects some years ago, including a collection of Walt Kelly's *Pogo* books. A page had dropped open, and there it was. He wished he had kept the book. Bob caught himself doodling. He focused again.

Why is it different to create a benchmark for fixed incomes and equities? Again, you tie it all to the asset allocation. In the world of fixed-income there's corporate fixed income and high yield, and different kinds of high yield benchmarks.
[SEE NOTE 6-2]

Bob studied his pad, seeing but not reading, reading but not perceiving. He had had it for the day.

"Come on, Molly," he called. "Walkies!"

The word grabbed the shih-tzu's attention, waking her up, but it failed to get her to her feet.

"Leash, Molly, leash!" She was out of the study in moments, her nails sliding on tiles en route to the door.

"O.K., girl. You're in for a real treat. We're going to discuss the importance of benchmarks, and risk and reward. You like rewards."

Sue was no longer in the sitting room. Bob called up the stairs. "We're away, Sue. Back in half an hour."

"O.K.," she called back. "Don't ask too much of that dog."

"I'll go easy on her." Bob grabbed his parka from the cupboard, reached in the usual left-hand outer pocket and found a sufficient supply of Kibbles. "Here's a reward, Molly. Good dog."

They clattered down the steps and out to the sidewalk

with Molly still chewing. "Maybe I'll set up a hedge-fund called Molly," he told her, "You'd like that, wouldn't you? We could invest in dog food futures!"

Molly was thoroughly in command, trotting ahead on her expanding cord.

"Where was I? Oh yes, benchmarks. When you look at high yield, Molly—and I hope you will—if you have your high yield allocation around the double-B grade, well, that's just one or two ratings under investment grade, which is triple-B and higher…" Bob stopped and his voice shut down. Feeling the restraint, Molly turned, sat down, and looked at him.

"I can see this might not make a whole lot of sense to you, Molly," Bob said softly, enjoying the fresh air. "Just try to take this in. At some remove from your woolly little head this alphabet soup of words I'm spouting pays for your food and your light, heat and vet bills, Moll." Bob bent down and gave her head a vigorous rubbing. "Talking to you helps me stay sane."

Mad with delight, Molly rolled on her back in the powder of snow.

"For heaven's sake, you dumb brute, not here!" The wriggling dog left the impression on the sidewalk of a snow-angel shaped like an over-sized bow tie.

Bob stood up, and so did Molly.

"The point I'm making is: If you're going to mix your assets, you cannot—repeat, *cannot*—even within discrete asset classes, use an overall high yield benchmark. You have to use sub-sectors that fit with what you are doing. No shortcuts! Hey, Moll!"

The tsih-tzu was away in the bushes, attacking smells, sounds and imagined prey. Bob had dropped her leash and she was dragging it around. He caught sight of the red, retractable handle bouncing erratically and got his foot on it.

"Gotcha!" He stuck the handle over a stub of branch to anchor it, traced along the cord, and gathered up his dog. "Come on, Molly. I'm taking you home." Bob felt a twinge of anxiety.

Sometimes it came unannounced. It wasn't always rational. In fact it was downright crazy to feel anxious. From time to time Bob made a list of every material and spiritual comfort he owned. It helped no end to ease the pain of the one thing he lacked: a job.

"What's your benchmark, Molly? From this point I'd guess one of them would be the hydrant, another one might be the end of our drive."

He threaded through the bushes cautiously, recalling a time almost twenty years ago when he and his classmates had trained in maneuvers and field craft in the woods on the steep basalt hills looming above the Hudson Valley and West Point.

"Let's take you home, kiddo." Bob set the shih-tzu down on the sidewalk and followed her lead. "I want to get this off my chest, Moll, and you're the best old-fashioned Dictaphone I got. Here goes:

"In the equity sector," he told her, "you find you have the same sort of issues. If you invest in high cap growth stocks, then the S&P 500 is a good measure for that because it deals in large caps. But there are other sub-indices that let you slice and dice, so you can compare against different sub-sectors.

"It's the same thing for hedge funds and so on, the whole purpose being to match as closely as possible the risk and reward of your asset allocation to the benchmark you choose. It doesn't have to be exotic. Just that dumb ol' off-the-shelf benchmark." [SEE NOTE 6-3]

Bob was wearing down. These weeks had been a strain, for Sue as well, and the time would undoubtedly stretch longer. They were both careful to be mutually supportive, behaving in some ways like newly-weds again.

"Here, Moll!" Man and dog had passed the familiar patch of woods. To their right a park stretched back from the road. Not far away, a mature tree offered cover for a snow-dusted bench. Bob cleared light snow with the back of a glove and sat down.

Molly jumped up beside him.

"You've got me wondering, Moll." Bob fluffed the dog's head. "There were so many reasons! A regular guy like me plays the game right down the middle, textbook pure, and then some dumb-ass comes along, all hat and no cattle, and pretty soon the raiders take the company and grab control. Maybe towards the end there was that benchmark I set too high because," he sighed, "because the board and the suits asked me to. Were they showing off for the business press and the analysts in the run-up to sale? Was I too optimistic? Too eager to please? Whatever, I left myself open, Moll. We were playing corporate games and, as I tell my students, when you're dealing with investments, everybody has a finger in the recipe of what a Chief Investment Officer wants to do.

"It was that collective 'we' that set the bar too high. Unreasonable expectations duly rewarded. Ignorance upstairs. Too much faith, hope and zero charity. Or was it inattention on my part? Anyway, I took the rap."

"We took a hit, Moll," Bob told the dog. "No worse than many. And my track record? Better than most, no damn' doubt about it! We hit a down-tick in the business, but the suits ran for cover!"

Molly seemed curiously attentive to this monologue, her ear cocked to make sense of the words she understood.

"Years ago, Molly, before you were old enough to chase squirrels, there lived a guy in Washington D.C. called Allen Dulles, a kindly grandfather type who smoked a pipe and rang the cash register in an oddball government store called the C.I.A.

"Well, one day a big tall customer in stripey pants and a matching stovepipe hat came in and whispered in Mr. Dulles's ear. Well, that got Mr. Dulles searching in the backroom through the sieves, the buckshot, dry goods, meat-grinders, horse collars, snake oil, black powder, zinc bath tubs and coils of rope until he found what his customer was looking for. It took a while, but Mr. Dulles laid his hand on just the right commodity, a little thing called 'plausible deniability.' That's where that expression comes from, Moll.

"And I know darn well that's what our board was looking for. Plausible deniability. The more you pay the suits the faster they duck and cover. Having been well-paid masters of indifference and indecision they suddenly woke up and took it out on me. Here, Moll, have a munchie. And then we'll take you home."

CHAPTER NOTES

An investment benchmark is what you could invest in if you did not have the services of an 'active' manager.

NOTE 6-1

An investment benchmark is what you could invest in if you did not have the services of an 'active' manager. Of course, passive investments, like index funds or exchange traded funds designed to mirror indices, can also be benchmarked to their related index. But, this will only provide an idea of how far off the passive fund is from the index it is trying to mimic.

An investment manager should not be trying to mimic the benchmark. A manager that does so, either inadvertently or purposefully, is often called a 'closet benchmarker'. Mention that to any active manager and they will immediately become concerned, to say the least. For if they are 'closet benchmarking,' why do you need to pay their management fee—and, quite frankly, their justification for existence would be seriously impaired. In all instances, he or she should be trying to 'beat' the benchmark, adjusted for risk. We will discuss judging manager performance in a later chapter.

Before beginning to develop a benchmark, we must get back to basics. What are the basic components of an appropriate benchmark?
1. Unambiguous – The securities that make up the benchmark should be publicly known.
2. Investable – Securities in the benchmark should include those that the investment manager can actually buy according to the policy.
3. Measurable – Benchmark returns should be something that can

NOTE 6-1

easily be quoted, since they are based upon prices of securities that are reliably determined.

4. Appropriate – It should be representative of the underlying investment universe. In other words, how similar is the benchmark to that which the portfolio can be comprised?
5. Reflective of Current Investment Opinions – The benchmark should be tied directly to the investment strategy.
6. Specified in advance – Importantly, the benchmark should be specified prior to measuring investment manager performance against it.

Thus, it is obvious that an appropriate benchmark must be customized. And, this customization should be directly related to the asset allocation decided upon in Chapter 3. Remember that the asset allocation is tied to the overall risk management of the insurer, including the risk/reward profile of liabilities.

Unfortunately, those who tout liability-based benchmarks—developing benchmarks directly from estimated liability cash flows—have probably never spent time in senior management of an insurance company. An insurer is much more than its liabilities: concerns such as new business, surplus levels, return on surplus, net income per accounting standards, rating agency concerns, etc.—all must be considered within the overall risk management approach noted in an earlier chapter.

NOTE 6-1

For example, if the asset allocation—this includes the impact of all relevant factors including the risk appetite of the insurer—determines that the company should have a fixed income portfolio with a duration of four years, then the benchmark—however it ends up looking—should have that duration.

If the investment strategy derived from that asset allocation tells us that we should focus on yield—adjusted for risk—more than total return, then the benchmark should contain fixed-income sectors that have more yield in them. Thus, for many insurers, a customized benchmark would have a very small proportion (if at all) in lower yielding US Treasuries and unsecured US Agency debt. Instead custom benchmarks tend to have higher proportions from 'spread sectors' than are found in the typical broad fixed income indices, like the Barclay's Capital Aggregate Index.

The art of developing a customized benchmark, then, must include determining which sectors make up the benchmark and to what proportion, taking into account that spread sectors will impact duration and convexity (interest rate risk), credit risk, liquidity risk, etc. And, it is important to consider all of these risks when developing a useful customized benchmark.

Thankfully, the broad indices are already decomposed by the index providers. Thus, the Barclay's Aggregate is easily divided into

NOTE 6-1

different sectors, durations within many of those sectors, even credit rating levels in some instances. Of course, these 'slices and dices' of the broad index may or may not allow us complete flexibility in developing a customized benchmark, but, in many instances they adequately meet the challenge.

But, what about a yield-based benchmark—one customized, yet focused on maintaining a given book yield and then compared to the managed portfolio's yield? We have seen many attempts at this, and two things seem clear.

First, yield-based benchmarks are incredibly complex to maintain and must contain arbitrary reinvestment rules.

Second, and most importantly, neither the yield in the benchmark nor the yield in the portfolio contain an allowance for various risks. For example, at no point does the yield on a corporate bond tell us the probability that we will not receive full return of principal. The yield is merely a measure of return on principal before adjustment for risk.

Some investment managers have devoted significant amounts of time and dollars in developing a yield-based benchmark. We believe that the result has been an interesting marketing approach with few direct benefits for the insurer. In fact, over-reliance on such contrived benchmarks can result in incorrect conclusions about manager

NOTE 6-1

performance—with the related problems in the overall investment process.

So, the bottom line is, do not be fooled by yield-based benchmarks. But, what should an insurer do if investment income is more important than total return?

We believe the answer is to have a properly constructed customized total return benchmark and an investment income benchmark. The manager should be aware of both and, as discussed in the chapter on performance management, deviations in return and risk-adjusted return should be explained and analyzed, while deviations in investment income can be explained by good old fashioned rate/volume analyses as noted in a later chapter.

Thus, investment benchmarking might seem simple at first, but indeed does have several key issues that must be considered. And these issues must also be able to be successfully communicated to senior management, the Board, the investment staff and, most importantly, the portfolio managers and/or external investment manager.

However, when it comes to communication, it pays to keep things simple, so perhaps Bob's dog could help us put some of this in perspective?

NOTE 6-2

Insurers look to investment grade (core) fixed income bond portfolios as a source of income as well as total return. Thus, custom benchmarks must be constructed that take this into account. However, other insurer investments are typically considered sources of long term growth. Thus, when it comes to high yield investments, the benchmark is typically a total return benchmark. It could be based upon a specific credit rating sub sector of the market, for example BB rated bonds. Or, it could be limited to exclude or limit the size of certain issuers' bonds in the benchmark, if the size of those issuers' bonds is unusually large and would tend to skew the benchmark returns one way or another.

Equity benchmarks can be generic in nature, such as the S&P 500 index, or could be tied to a certain style or market capitalization. For example, a manager or fund that is being utilized for its style of investment in mid-cap growth companies, would have a benchmark that was a mid-cap growth benchmark. Such flexibility is made possible by the myriad of benchmark style and capitalization characteristics offered by indices produced by Standard and Poor's or other competing benchmark index firms.

NOTE 6-3

Or, to put it another way, benchmarking is something that nobody should take for granted. But, it is something that will greatly influence the investment manager's style and strategy. No manager wants to stray too far from the benchmark, lest she risk material underperformance and the loss of the mandate. Thus, we hear managers typically say, 'we try to hit singles, not home runs,' a nice way of saying 'we will track the benchmark, but please don't call us closet indexers.'

To construct an appropriate benchmark for the insurer, we must start with the strategic asset allocation. For example, the core fixed income benchmark is directly related to the asset allocation chosen by the insurer. Thus, a core fixed income customized benchmark would start with the broad core fixed income benchmark, say the Barclays Aggregate, but then re-weight sectors to be similar to the preferred asset allocation. In most instances this will mean a benchmark with investments in fewer Treasuries and Agencies than the Aggregate, but with more spread sector bonds (corporates, mortgages, etc). The result is that the market yield of the custom benchmark would be greater than that of the Aggregate index, while still maintaining adherence to duration targets. Here is just one example of how a custom benchmark might look like and compare to the Aggregate index.

NOTE 6-3

Custom Benchmark	Agg Weighting %	Custom Benchmark Weighting %	Yld to Worst	Duration
Barclays Capital MBS Index	38.0%	35.0%	4.19	2.89
Barclays Capital Credit Index	23.2%	35.0%	5.06	6.14
Barclays Capital ABS AAA-Rated Index	0% *	5.0%	4.04	3.16
Barclays Capital Agency Index	10.6%	10.0%	2.33	3.44
Barclays Capital Treasury Index	25.5%	10.0%	2.34	5.17
Barclays Capital CMBS, Eligible for Agg Index, AAA only	0% **	5.0%	7.75	4.01
Custom Benchmark		100.0%	4.29	4.38
Barclays Capital Aggregate Bond Index			3.88	4.31

Notes:
* Total ABS Index 0.48% of aggregate
** Total CMBS Index 3.44% of aggregate

Note that the custom benchmark and the Aggregate have similar duration, yet the custom benchmark has a considerable advantage in market yield.

It doesn't stop there. After putting together a benchmark, one must determine if the manager's behavior is likely to be influenced in a way that is consistent with the preferred strategic asset allocation as well as the company's key goals and objectives.

The result from a proper custom fixed income benchmark will be manager behavior in concert with the overall investment process.

UNCERTAIN TIMES | 125

NOTE 6-3

However, benchmarks provide total return comparisons, not accounting related information. And, that is where issues like credit impairments can also make a huge impact in determining how the investment process is judged.

7

WHOSE CALL IS IT, ANYWAY?

INVESTMENT MANAGEMENT, RESPONSIBILITY AND EVALUATION

Bob held the door for Sue, blew a kiss after she got in the car and watched her back out of the drive, leaving him with Sarah. She would be half an hour at the market, at least.

He went to his study and picked up the phone. This was a call he had wanted to make for a week. Not that it demanded privacy. It was just that he didn't know what he might be forced to say.

He dialed a local number. "Jeremy?"

"Yeah?"

"Bob Short here."

"Hey, buddy, long time no hear from. How ya doing?"

"Let's just say this is a networking call."

"Uh-oh. What happened?"

"I got fired."

Silence from the other end spoke volumes. And posed questions.

Bob moved swiftly to explain why he was calling. "I'm gearing up to get back in the job market. I'd appreciate a debriefing with you, Jem."

"Any time, boy. Still play chess?"

"Some."

"Yea, yea. I'll beat your ass again in return for a slice of my know-how. How's that strike you?"

"Good, Jem."

A pause at the other end of the line suggested rapid mental calculations. "I'm on the wagon! You know that. But there's no reason why you shouldn't have a drink. I'm one guy who loves watching other people drink alone! So come to my place. No point talking business over there and upsetting Sue. I'll set up the board. Hey, I'll even let you play white. And I'll still whip you!"

They made a date, and Bob put down the phone, feeling a whole lot better.

The only thing these men had in common was the United States Army. Jeremy Libertz was fifteen years older than Bob. He had come up through the ranks the hard way but, being a natural fixer he had wangled his way through the Army's Quartermaster School at Fort Lee, Virginia. In his prime—which included a spell with Bob in the 24th Mechanized Infantry Division—there was nothing that Jeremy Libertz hadn't been able to fix, find or obtain. After Jem's stint with the service came a pension, work in finance and a couple of ventures that spun a bit of money. For Jem it seemed effortless.

They met a few evenings later. Bob took the elevator to the seventh floor of a downtown condo and rang the bell. Jeremy answered the door. He reminded Bob of the actor Telly Savalas—bulky, with a ready smile, a fast retort, and not much hair. Bob could see in the background he already had the chessboard set up. It had been a while since they met, so they took a few minutes to catch up. Then they sat at the side table where Jem had placed the game.

"Hey," Jeremy exclaimed, as the lines of chessmen triggered a thought. "I recall you had a fetish about two Persian brothers and a Greek guy. See, I remember that lecture you gave us about Cunaxa—along with our operational briefing plan!"

"The Greek guy, Xenophon, led two thousand mercenaries back from Persia to Greece."

"Nothing that guy couldn't do! Should have been a quartermaster. I'll play Mr. X, and I'll be black." Jem turned the board to place the white pieces in front of Bob. "You still angry, Bob?"

"Angry?"

"About losing that job."

"Yeah, some."

"Some? I'd be sore for sure. Listen, Bob, I'm sorry I steered you to it. You're too level-headed to play with hysterics."

"Hysterics?"

"They're running scared. You set the bar high, Bob. O.K., you missed a few. The way the market is right now you're well out of it. They're in trouble. What did Greening say to you?"

"D'you know, I don't remember zilch. It was like I was sitting there and he was flapping his lips. A silent movie."

"Yea, the worse the news... You're playing white, Bob. It's your move."

[MOVE 1#1: Bob advanced his king's pawn two squares to e4.]

Jem teased him for it. "Traditionalist, eh?"

"I'm going to call him, Jem."

"Who, Greening? Why?"

"To try and get him to repeat what he said. Why was I fired?"

"Don't waste your time. He invented it that day. He'll make it up again." *[MOVE 1#2: Jeremy waved his own king's pawn at Bob before moving it forward two squares, to e5.]* "Get a grip, Bob! The portfolio went down. They had to look blameless.

Yours were the entrails they had to inspect."

"Hey, Jem…"

"I'm not kidding. Listen, you told me you chose the investment manager. I don't recall the name."

"Greening said I was responsible it hadn't worked out."

"Ah, it's coming back to you! You just forgot to push Play! Who hired the investment manager?"

"I guess I did."

"What do you mean, you *guess* you did?"

"Greening chaired the committee that passed my recommendation to the board. Unanimous. Suddenly the market turned south and I was wearing the wrong hire." [SEE NOTE 7-1]

Jeremy clicked his teeth. "Were you flying solo when you made that hire?"

"They made it seem that way." *[MOVE 2#1: Bob advanced his knight to f3.]*

Jem responded, "Good move, kiddo. I taught you chess too well. If I don't respond to that move, you'll take my pawn, so you've forced me to set my own plans back. What were your assets under management, Bob?"

"Just under a billion."

"Let me see if I still connect. From a practical standpoint, once you hit a billion the company gets to thinking: 'Should we go for some or all internal management?'"

"You don't forget much, Jem. If you're under a billion, the easy way is to take your short-term portfolio and maybe your Treasuries and Agencies and manage them internally."

"And why not? There's no or very little credit risk." *[MOVE 2#2: Jeremy advanced his queen's pawn to d6, protecting his other exposed pawn against Bob's knight.]*

"And no negative convexity. You pick your benchmark and manage to that. But then it gets sticky. As your assets under management rise past a billion, management wants more hands-on control, so they tend to hire internal investment managers."

"Doesn't always work, Bob."

"I know that. What they gain in comfort level, they lose in expertise. I argued for keeping a lot of assets under external management."

"How so?"

"There's a huge advantage staying external from the standpoint of resources and expertise that's available out there. External managers have contacts and expertise across a market spectrum that long-term in-house employees just can't touch."
[SEE NOTE 7-2]

[MOVE 3#1: Bob advanced his queen's pawn to d4.]

"Ha! I see you're setting up a struggle for the middle of the board, Bob. As for your external managers—I get it! You kept the company's assets out there to benefit from their external experience. You gave Greening and those guys your all."

" 'Experience' wasn't the word that came back. The word Greening used was 'exposure.' "

"You played the good soldier and lost, Bob."

"Funny you mention "good soldier." We had an instructor at the Academy who made us look at the Army from the bottom up, and the outside looking in, on the theory that any self-managing organization can make a fool of itself unless it's careful."

"Oh, sure, you bet!"

She gave us readings from a classic written by a Czech at the time of the First World War. Depending how you look at institutions, *The Good Soldier Schweik* is either a real hoot or a tragic object lesson. It's great satire. The author was taking apart his own Austro-Hungarian Army, but his book points out how people in complex organizations compound the errors they make in proportion to their status in the hierarchy."

"There's a mouthful! I think what you mean is: the higher they go, the more they screw up and the more they get paid to screw up! More scotch, Bob?"

"No, Jem. I'm driving."

[MOVE 3#2: Jeremy ran his bishop across the board to g4.] Moments later he thought better of it. "Damn!"

"What's the matter, Jem?"

"I just made my first mistake. I'm screwing around to save a pawn!"

"In my humble opinion, I think that's what Greening did—while implying that was what I had done. I think he remarked that my management style created either 'needless' or 'adverse' exposure. Maybe both. Meaning: the results I got from external management didn't justify our exposure—in one sector of the portfolio."

"Was he right?"

"Not in my opinion."

"If you won't have more scotch, how about straight soda?"

"Sure. Half a glass, Jem."

Jeremy poured, asking, "And when everyone ran for cover?"

" 'Stuff happens,' to quote the immortal words."

"Sounds like *The Good Soldier* ought to be taught in business school!"

"Well, the Czech language adopted the term 'to *schweik*.' You stick it on the front of another word to imply stupidity or subversion wherever it falls."

"Which doesn't help you get work, especially with *schweiks*!"

"That's right."

"Going to set up as a consultant?"

"I gotta settle my head first, Jem. You can't be angry in business."

"No. Don't let it morph into depression, boy."

They lapsed into silence until Bob pushed a piece across the board. *[MOVE 4#1: Bob slid his pawn from d4 to take Jem's on d5.]*

"Hah, first blood! But why would you take a pawn to lose a

knight?" *[MOVE 4#2: Jem slid his bishop one diagonal space to f3, taking Bob's knight.]*

Bob sat fixedly staring at the board.

"If you do set up as a consultant," Jem added at length, "I hope I'll be in a position to send stuff your way."

"Thanks for the offer. I appreciate that." *[MOVE 5#1: Bob advanced his queen to take Jem's bishop.]*

"Oho! I thought you'd use your pawn for that. You're making your lady work for her living, Bob." *[MOVE 5#2: Jem nudged his pawn to d4, taking Bob's.]* "Tell me about external investment managers these days."

"Sounds like you're looking for work yourself, Jem."

"No. I like to keep up. Besides, if I'm going to help you I'll have to catch up with the minefield out there."

Bob considered Jem the sort of guy who wouldn't be phased by passing through a minefield: he had the sort of luck that would bring him out in one piece.

Now he brought Jem up to date. "Here's how it sizes up. When a company gets its managed assets up to five or six hundred million, it starts to ask itself: Is one external manager enough? That's almost a knee-jerk reaction. Let's say the company has its asset allocation balanced—but here's the rub. If it's going to go for an external manager, it better balance that manager's expertise to match its existing allocation. You need specialists for equities, and I don't have to tell you high yield bonds..."

Jem cut him short, "They're tricky stuff!"

[MOVE 6#1: Bob moved his king-side bishop to c4,] giving him two threatening pieces to move against Jem, whose game was beginning to lag. "Trouble is, Jem, when you recruit additional external managers to suit your asset allocations, you multiply your costs."

"You can also get the cart before the horse."

"How so?"

"Plain old inertia. If you're not real careful, you might let the asset allocation slide to fit the external managers you have in place."

"Right. Never give your horse its rein!"

[MOVE 6#2: With unintended irony, Jem moved his knight to f6, stalling Bob's advance.] "Any other issues, Bob?"

"Oh yes. First you have to *find* those managers."

"Has that changed any since my day?"

"These days we call it the '4 Ps' approach."

"Such as?"

"Philosophy, process, people, performance." [SEE NOTE 7-3]

" 'Philosophy' means how does the asset management firm manage your investment portfolio? How active are their managers going to be? What's their value-added? Do they turn it over a lot and make up the cost of turnovers with additional returns? *[MOVE 7#1: Bob moved his queen to b3, giving him a direct line on two pawns, and threatening a strike on a knight.]*

" 'Process' means just that. What is an external company's management process? Where do their decisions start? How often do they meet, and how many players? How do they transmit their decisions to their portfolio managers and traders? How long does that take, and who checks? How much do they plug their client in to their internal channels of communication? Finally, do they work hard at making a good marriage: does their manager connect well with the insurer? That integrates with a lot of 'People' issues here.

" 'People' of course is: how expert in handling *insurance* assets are the folks at the asset management firm?

Jem responded, "Makes sense!" adding, "You forgot one thing. How well does a management company treat its own managers?" He studied the board, seeming to make heavy weather of his strategy. He shook his head, "Tsk, tsk, tsk," pausing a moment before he moved. *[MOVE 7#2: Jem slapped his queen down on e7.]*

Bob added color commentary, "The best move you could have made."

"Either you're getting better," Jem retorted, "or I'm getting worse!"

"Believe me, Jem, I've had more practice positioning myself than you have these past weeks."

"Not very successfully before they kicked you out, by the sound of it. But I bet you got the message now!" Studying the board, Jem shook his head. "You were telling me about the letter P, Bob."

"Yes. The '4 Ps' approach." The last P is 'Performance': That relates to searching and hiring managers. What I found effective was sticking like glue to a specific timeline and hiring schedule."

Jem nodded. "I know what you're going to say. I had a fight with human resources some years ago. We were losing too much time because the client's CEO's brother-in-law or some such person wanted onto the candidate list."

"There are always one or two like that. And a short answer, Jem. If you're contracted to do a manager search, you have to give your client a deadline to submit names. When that time expires, get on with the selection."

"I'm guessing that stress levels have ratcheted up."

"Oh yeah. To warp speed. On both sides." *[MOVE 8#1: Bob moved his knight to c3.]*

Jem responded: "I see you've decided to strangle me slowly. You're a slow developer, Bob. You could have played your bishop or your queen."

"I enjoy your company, Jem."

"Tsk, tsk. Listen, kiddo. I know something about stress, and I'd guess you had a belly-full before and after you were fired. You've had your share of negotiating management fees, eh, Bob?"

"It's no end of grief. Life would be simpler if you could bring managers onto staff. But that takes us back to where we were: you don't get the additional expertise you get from external managers." Bob contemplated his empty glass before adding quietly, "And even they can screw up."

Jem played host, adding soda to Bob's glass. "Hey," he said, "nobody gets ahead of a cosmic catastrophe." *[MOVE 8#2: Jem advanced his pawn to hinder Bob's knight.]* "The simple fact is, some time or another everybody gets to deal with a Greening in this world—a world in a mess. If they need an excuse and they want you out, you're out. Move on, boy. Churn your Bradley over him. Leave him eating dust. You'll go far, Bob. You don't need this."

"I hope so, Jem."

"Sure. Most managers don't get fired because they missed a benchmark. You know that. Most managers, and I mean *most*, get fired because there are a host of factors including poor communication with the client."

"*I* was the client!"

"Nah, I meant your internal client. You gave somebody an excuse to take a second look and find a fault that suited them—right then and there. Currently the searches I'm hearing about go like this: Performance is important, but there are a lot of other drivers, and communications is up there near the top. With the investment world the way it is, can you blame them? If I had to sum it up I'd say the key priority, especially these days, is: keep your client in the loop, 'cause he'll have his eyes over your shoulder all the time. No surprises! Remember that!"

"I should do a training interview with you, Jem."

"Any time you're ready, Bob. If your interview technique is like your chess, you'll ace it."

"As long as a company is prepared to live with my policy! Above a certain point, anything complex needs external consultant resources. Unless you're largely into Treasuries and Agencies—and who is?—you need that expertise."

"How about ethics, Bob? Managers might churn your

portfolio to generate soft dollars or simply to beat the benchmark and collect an incentive based fee."

"Not the ones I hire, Jem. If you're hiring a manager to do the best job he can, why would you pay an incentive to do it? I've seen cases where incentive fees have really backfired. If a manager falls behind his benchmark he might stretch a portfolio until it's as risky as possible within the policy. A guy like that may even make good decisions economically, but he's taking them to make up ground. I'm not interested in hiring people who'd expose a portfolio to risk for no better reason than giving themselves the best chance for maximizing personal returns."

"That's got to be an act of desperation!"

"I'm not judging motive, but it happens." *[MOVE 9#1: Bob moved his bishop to g5.]*

Jem cracked his knuckles. "Hey, you pinned my knight! If I move my horse, I lose my queen."

"Let's just say you took the evening off, Jem! Try a Hail Mary pass—And, by the way, I've known managers who'll do that if they figure there's no down side. They're going to get their base fee, no matter what."

"Nah, no Hail Mary pass from me! Not tonight. I'm conceding defeat. It's your game, fair and square, Bob." Jeremy admitted defeat graciously, toppling his king in the time honored fashion.

"Thank you, Jem."

"What's your next step, kiddo?"

"It's called 'Do-as-you-would-be-done-by.' How do you set about evaluating managers? Well, that gets into benchmark stuff, but typically I would want to see three to five years worth of performance, of data, before I could begin to draw conclusions about someone else. And *that's* how I expect they'll judge me. I'm pulling all my stats together."

"You'll get there, Bob. You'll get there. You pull your stats together! You'll come out of this smelling like Mr. X stuck in a hard place. I got my faith in you." [SEE NOTE 7-4]

7
CHAPTER NOTES

It sounds as if Bob may have erred in the execution of the investment manager search...

NOTE 7-1

It sounds as if Bob may have erred in the execution of the investment manager search, but many do. Sometimes such errors are irrelevant, as when an appropriate and successful investment manager relationship is forged. However, sometimes errors only surface after the manager has been hired.

For virtually all insurers, searching for and hiring a new investment manager is something they rarely do. And, that means the most important part of the investment manager search is having an agreed-upon plan for it. As we have noted earlier, the key to investment success is having a solid investment process. Thus, the key to a successful manager search is having a solid process for that search.
Steps employed in such a search are sometimes glossed over or combined, but they truly require attention to detail. Sometimes, pressure of daily activity causes things to be missed, or sometimes someone may not be fully aware of every procedural detail. We tend to lead the manager search process through nine basic steps, which involve some of these questions:

1. Determine the company's initial preferences and how best to conduct the search. This sets the tone for the entire process and goes well past 'we just want to find a core fixed-income manager.' What kind of manager? Any preference for size? Insurance expertise level? Location? (Some companies want the security-blanket feel of having a manager within driving dis-

NOTE 7-1

tance.) And, who will be making decisions throughout the process? How will the Board, Investment Committee, or others be involved in the process—and when might they be involved?

2. Set criteria for manager selection. What are some of the characteristics the company likes/dislikes in its current manager? What are some of the capabilities approaches, etc, that the company would like to see the selected manager have?

3. Screen for an initial list of candidates from a comprehensive database of investment managers. This is also where the company can decide to include or exclude specific managers. And, this is usually where, if it occurs, someone near and dear to the heart of a Board member gets added to the list of candidates. It is important that all candidates be put on a 'level playing field' for comparison purposes. And, as the process continues the Board member will be able to tell someone like his brother- in-law that they were given full consideration, but that his firm compared poorly with better qualified candidates. Thus political—and familial—cover is provided for all.

You will also notice the use of a "comprehensive database of investment managers." This is important: just because a manager has been buying you lunch, golf or other enticements, it does not mean that his firm would be best for the

NOTE 7-1

assignment. You can usually gain access to such databases at investment consulting firms. Our firm maintains its own proprietary database of managers with insurance specialization, since this is, in most cases, a requirement for most insurers. Thus, it is important that you can consider all possible candidates at this early stage—and that means you must start with a fairly deep database of possibilities.

4. Develop and transmit a confidential company-specific questionnaire to obtain from the candidates the answers to questions important to your company. What are the key issues you face managing the portfolio? How would the prospective manager handle those issues? A good investment consultant can also help you identify issues, as well as raise others you will need to consider in the new investment manager relationship.

5. Recommend a final list of three to four managers to the company. Develop and transmit an additional questionnaire, if necessary, to further refine manager responses.

There are many different tools that you can use to review and 'score' responses from candidates. One of the tools we like is a Pugh Matrix. It allows for weighting various characteristics, scoring a candidate manager on that characteristic in comparison to the incumbent and then developing a weighted

NOTE 7-1

score that can be used to filter the top candidates for more detailed 'finalist' reviews.

The Pugh Matrix was invented by Stuart Pugh at the University of Strathclyde in Glasgow, Scotland. Pugh designed it as an approach for evaluating multiple options against each other, relative to baseline options.

The process for developing a Pugh Matrix is fairly straightforward. First, identify the relevant user requirements. These can be tied to the questionnaire for the managers or simply to a list of key characteristics. Second, develop weights for each of those characteristics. We typically use a 1-5 scale, but any relevant scale will do. Third, generate several alternatives. That is what the earlier steps in the manager search process have been all about. These are the managers you are considering. Fourth, select one of the alternatives as a baseline. That alternative is usually the incumbent manager for comparison purposes. Fifth, evaluate each manager-alternative against the datum (the baseline manager) for each of the characteristics. In that evaluation, determine if the manager alternative is better (+), the same (S), or worse (-) versus the baseline manager for each characteristic. In our analyses, we typically expand these to include double pluses (++) and double minuses (--). For each manager alternative, determine the weighted pluses and

NOTE 7-1

minuses to develop a weighted score. Positive weighted scores indicate the manager alternative to be better than the baseline manager.

Like any decision grid, the Pugh Matrix can be manipulated. So, an honest appraisal is very important to the use of the Matrix. In fact, we would recommend that each alternative manager be considered without reference to any manager other than the baseline. To add a degree of consistency in the decision making, we would also recommend that the Matrix be reviewed a second time to make certain everyone providing input and opinions feel secure in their assessments.

Here is what a Pugh Matrix looks like. In this example, it appears that Manager C has the highest rating primarily because of its superiority in Criteria 3. Of course, Managers A and B are also better than the current manager (status quo), so all are potentially worth further review and subsequent rescoring of the Pugh Matrix.

NOTE 7-1

Legend:
- **- -** Disadvantage compared to the status quo (2X's as bad)
- **-** Disadvantage compared to the status quo (1X as bad)
- **s** No advantage / disadvantage to the status quo
- **+** Better than the status quo (1X better)
- **++** Better than the status quo (2X's better)

	Key Criteria:	Importance Rating	Status Quo	Manager A	Manager B	Manager C
1	Criteria 1	4	s	+	-	s
2	Criteria 2	4	s	-	-	s
3	Criteria 3	5	s	-	-	+
4	Criteria 4	5	s	+	+	+
5	Criteria 5	3	s	s	s	-
6	Criteria 6	5	s	s	s	s
7	Criteria 7	3	s	+	+	s
8	Criteria 8	5	s	s	+	+
9	Criteria 9	3	s	s	s	+
10	Criteria 10	4	s	s	s	-
11	Criteria 11	3	s	s	s	-
	Sum of positives		0	3	4	4
	Sum of double positives		0	0	0	0
	Sum of negatives		0	3	3	3
	Sum of double negatives		0	0	0	0
	Sum of sames		11	5	4	4
	Weighted sum of positives		0	14	16	18
	Weighted sum of double positives		0	0	0	0
	Weighted sum of negatives		0	12	13	10
	Weighted sum of double negatives		0	0	0	0
	Total weighted sum		0	2	3	8

NOTE 7-1

6. Manager finalist presentations. Here the 'finalist' managers, usually three to four, get to strut their stuff for the Investment Committee or similar decision-making body. However, it is important that this not become a beauty contest or just an opportunity for the managers to provide their usual marketing palaver. The managers should be instructed to speak specifically to issues identified in advance by the insurance company. This may include providing initial portfolio recommendations, addressing certain credit issues, or other topics of interest. The managers should also be instructed to limit the time they get to tell the Committee how great a firm they are. At this stage of the process, all finalists should be worthy of the mandate under consideration. So, they all are 'great' in their own way and it is more important to spend a very directed one to 1.5 hours on issues that directly impact the insurance company.

It is in these finalist presentations that a manager considered a 'front runner' in the Pugh Matrix may reveal itself to be less appropriate than another finalist manager. That is why the Pugh Matrix is an excellent tool, but it is no substitute for in-person meetings with the candidate managers.

During the finalist presentations, we recommend that time be pre-scheduled between presentations that will allow the Committee to talk about their impressions and thoughts. In this way, one allocates time after all presentations to discussing

NOTE 7-1

which managers should be considered for further consideration, or, in the best case, a choice or choices can be made.

Although most insurance companies can handle this phase with ease, the experience of an investment consultant in this process—which a consultant repeats many times a year—can be invaluable. The consultant can provide background on what he has seen before in similar situations and if the candidate management firms are sticking to the same story given another insurer. They can also help provide perspective and read between the lines of what the manager is saying... and not saying.

7. Perform on-site due diligence visits. Although some insurers may want to skip this step, it can be quite instructive to perform an on-site visit to a manager's offices either before or after the finalist presentations.

We have been to a lot of finalist presentations and many more due diligence visits. The first rule of those visits is to not make it into a social outing. The manager will want to schmooze as much as possible in order to make the insurer's senior management feel comfortable that the manager is 'our kind of people'. But, 'our kind of people' may not have the resources to truly meet the requirements of the insurer.

NOTE 7-1

During the on-site visit, the insurer will be shown the manager's trading floor (if you've seen one, you've seen them all...really, they just vary in size and electronics), meet the key people at the firm and discuss various issues about the portfolio, markets, etc. Unplanned, these visits can really become more of a sales pitch and less of a detailed review of issues that should be revisited.

For a productive meeting, we recommend some advance planning and starting with the end in mind. What do you want to get out of these meetings? What are some of the unanswered questions that arose from the finalist presentations? Who do you want to see at the firm and what questions should they answer? Do you want to see certain market sector specialists, investment strategists, etc.? Do you want to meet the manager's CEO in order to get a better handle on the firm's consistency of ownership, etc (mergers and acquisitions continue to run rampant throughout the investment management industry)? These are just a few questions to consider.

8. Negotiate acceptable fees. External investment managers will admit to core fixed-income fees well below those they could charge non-insurers—and yet insurer accounts require much more work than a typical pension account. However, they will also admit that insurers tend to be much slower to make changes than those non-insurers, like pension funds. Thus,

NOTE 7-1

investment management firms hope that the lower fees are offset by long-term relationships. And, for most insurers, the desire is for a long-term, successful relationship, since making changes can be time consuming and costly. But, why are core fixed income management fees lower for insurer assets? It is how the market has evolved. In contrast to pension funds and other discrete pools of assets, an insurer's is an ongoing business with a focus on overall financial management of the enterprise, and that includes the bottom line. And the only thing 100% certain about an investment management relationship is the amount of fees paid—that go directly against the bottom line.

9. Establish service standards, including specific expectations of the manager relationship.

This is perhaps the most vital step in the entire search process and yet it is often either glossed over or simply 'assumed' to be fine. It is very important to not only know who will be on the service team from the management firm, but also how often they will be required to attend in-person meetings. Establishing the correct amount and quality of communication flow is important. Will your company be speaking with the manager by phone weekly, monthly, daily, etc? What level of discretion will truly be granted to the manager? Call before any buy or sell? Get permission before any transaction? Or, merely

NOTE 7-1

continue to manage the portfolio within policy limits against a stated benchmark? Or, do you set some other communications protocol?

Does the manager fully understand how he or she will be evaluated? Over what time periods and how? What are the expectations of senior management and the Board in this relationship? Discord in expectations between the company and the manager can and will eventually surface if those expectations are not clearly outlined and understood by all.

So, as you can see, performing a manager search is a detailed, complex process that must receive sufficient senior management involvement and 'buy-in' throughout. Shortcutting some of these steps is not recommended, or the result might be something similar to Bob's situation.

NOTE 7-2

Bob is correct in his assessment that a good external management firm should bring resources to the process that would be difficult to duplicate in any small or medium sized insurer. But, success in the investment management relationship is directly related to how the manager is managed.

Is the manager constantly challenged and questioned by the insurer? Does the insurer know the right questions to ask at the right time?

Too many times, insurer senior management teams are impressed by the investment manager they have hired—so impressed that they may seem hesitant to ask deep, probing questions, thinking that the manager knows best. But, the manager knows only what he can glean from the insurer. And, that means that open, honest, probing questions from both can serve to improve communications flow. The question becomes: Can the insurer successfully lever the deep resources of a good investment management firm to the full benefit of the insurance company? Doing so requires knowledge of what one knows and what one does not...

NOTE 7-3

The standard four P process has been around for decades and serves as an excellent backdrop for asking questions about manager candidates. Whether during the initial or subsequent questionnaire, subsequent interviews, or on-site visits, organizing one's inquiries around this basic approach can be quite rewarding. But, let's have Bob explain them in more detail.

NOTE 7-4

Bob is right about measuring the manager's performance against the benchmark, but in the insurance world that's only a part of the investment process that is typically reviewed at the end of each quarter or month. For all the other days of the year, monitoring what is going on in the portfolio becomes important, and that's what Bob will consider next.

8

DON'T CLOSE YOUR EYES!

KEEP YOUR PORTFOLIO ON A SHORT LEASH

Bob woke to find the bed empty beside him. Sue was already up and, by the sounds coming up from downstairs, she was feeding Molly. The back screen door clicked, followed by barking from the back yard as Molly welcomed the day.

Bob sprang out of bed, pulled his robe over pajamas, and went downstairs.

"You were late, last night," Sue said quietly, feigning nonchalance, and failing. "Where did you go?"

"To see an old army buddy."

She tried to hide it, but Bob could see her face fall. He could guess what was going through her head: she was imagining two guys feeling betrayed by life getting drunk.

Bob, leaning on the frame of the kitchen door, straightened up and approached her, saying quietly across the table, "You remember Jeremy Libertz. We played chess." Then, as an afterthought: "And I won."

Sue smiled back, "Oh, sure," breaking the tension.

"Jem was a natural fixer in the army and he's managed to survive in finance ever since. I called him to ask for advice."

"About business?"

"Uh-huh."

"Was it useful?"

"In the years I've known him, I've never heard Jeremy say a foolish word. As for last night's little chat, we'll have to wait and see."

If Bob's answer disappointed Sue, she didn't show it.

"I'm going to get dressed and do my notes for tonight's class," he told her. Bob had noticed that she seemed reassured when he made a habit of laying out his plan for the day. So now he did so every morning. "Oh, and by the way, I think I can write a 'How to' book after this course. But first, I'll feed the birds and …" Bob reacted to Molly imperiously barking at the back door, "... let the dog in."

Bob had noticed that he seemed to do his class notes best when Molly was in residence, snoring from time to time and interrupting her sleep to pace around his desk in a not so subtle search for handouts. Bob had developed the habit of trying out his thoughts on the dog before writing them down, although the quality of their intellectual repartee left much to be desired.

"Folks typically confuse portfolio monitoring and performance management in their minds," Bob announced across his desk. Molly didn't stir. "They may be connected, Moll, but never confuse the two!" The dog turned around in search of peace and quiet. Her wicker basket squeaked.

Bob sighed and picked up his pen to write: *Portfolio monitoring refers to keeping a really close eye on what's going on in your portfolio—especially when you receive reports that measure performance. It should be a key part of the job, whether the CIO does it personally or delegates the work to someone else.*

He carefully compiled his list:
- Portfolio monitoring:
- Compliance monitoring
- Investment practices review
- Analytical reporting review
- Communication process
- Stress and sensitivity testing
- Black swan events
- Changing regulatory or accounting environments
- Turnover analysis [SEE NOTE 8-1]

That evening, Bob let himself into the classroom, set down his projector and fired up his first slide, ready to go. He clicked through the first few images and stopped to review the content of the evening's class. He didn't have long to wait. His students soon arrived. Bill Hanna staggered back in mock horror. "Boy, you take no prisoners, Bob! That's some agenda."

Sally Prentice added, "In a tough course, too. Not that I'm complaining," she added hastily. "If I can ace this I'll be set for anything!"

Ken Stiller said nothing, just angled himself into a desk, studied the slide, linked his fingers behind his head and smiled: "Hi, Bob." He was evidently loosening up, feeling more comfortable with the others, too.

"Hi, Ken … Bill … Sally."

"Black swan events!" Bill was playing to the room. "I can hardly wait."

Bob took charge. "Don't rush me. Everything in its time. Everyone ready?"

Nobody objected, so he began: "I know it's bad form to have more than five bullet points on a slide. I've got eight and a hanger-on, but—hey, this is tough stuff. Let's get to grips with the whole setup, all at once. Anyone have any suggestions about compliance monitoring? What do we mean by that?"

Ken Stiller responded. "The term is ambiguous. It could refer to regulatory compliance, or to monitoring how well the portfolio is being managed within the policy."

"Good point, Ken. So let's be careful how we handle this phrase. In fact it takes us back to the first hour in this course. I'm referring to: How does the actual portfolio stand up to comparison with the investment policy limits and guideline? Yes, Sally?"

"You also have to make sure you have the right systems in place for pre-trade and post-trade compliance."

"Can you narrow that down?"

"You need to be sure you know the strategy and how it may or may not approach the limits of the guidelines and the policy."

"Exactly. That's the compliance part of it. You don't want to sail too close to the wind. [SEE NOTE 8-2]

"What's next?" Bob asked, rhetorically. " 'Investment practices review.' Anyone got anything to say?"

Bill responded, "Sounds obvious to me: What are the investment practices your managers have adopted and are they going to keep your baby on its tracks?"

"Thanks, Bill. Let's just add two thoughts to that setup. What are the investment practices your managers are using to implement the overall philosophy, and are they in tune with the spirit of the investment policy?"

Bill was puzzled: "What do you mean by 'spirit of the investment policy'? Are we talking ethics now?"

"No. This takes us back to the—oh, I don't know—maybe the first time we got together. Sally just mentioned this. Each and every investment policy needs its guiding principles. Remember we talked about risk profiles, the risk appetite expressed and approved by the board? Are the investment managers on the straight and narrow there? Are they living up to that? We have to check 'em out."

Bob had stopped using the teacher's podium. With just three

students he had adopted the sensible course of action, turning a desk around and inviting his students to form a circle. As they all got to know each other the course had become informal.

"Anyone want to add to 'Investment practices review'? he asked.

"Yes," said Sally. "You mentioned two points just now. What was the second?"

"Thanks for the reminder. The second is: The policy design may have looked great in theory. But how does it work in practice, and does it need adjustment? If it's not carrying its weight, you may have to consult the bosses and suggest revisions. O.K.?"

Sally nodded. "Thank you."

"You're welcome." [SEE NOTE 8-3]

"We move on. The next subhead: 'Analytical reporting review.' During each quarter, especially towards the end, managers should be reviewing risk reports. There are several competing analyses, listing securities down to the individual level. Now, here I raise points for discussion: Is this overkill, and how do you use these reports? How good is their information? Are they worthwhile?"

"We've just come through a period when—Shock! Horror!—the world has discovered rating agencies giving Triple-A status to junk," said Ken.

Sally added, "Meaning, can we trust any source of numbers or data any more?"

Bill continued Sally's thought, "I suppose if you subscribe to this risk management stuff it at least shows you're doing due diligence even if the most 'reputable' sources have been lying through their teeth."

"There speaks a real cynic!" said Ken. "I happen to agree with you, Bill. It's going to take a while before a modicum of trust comes back to roost, especially in the banking world."

Bob broke in: "Which brings me back to my point. With

respect to this aspect of risk management, how are we going to use it in investment management, both at the front line manager level, and at the senior level?"

Sally cut in. "Are those reports worthwhile?"

And Ken, "And is there enough in them to make them relevant to the specific needs of a company's portfolio?"

The three of them were looking to Bob for answers. He responded in mock horror: "Don't look at me! These are questions you're going to have to answer on the job—if you're lucky, you'll be working at it in more settled times."

Bill Hanna took a shot at an answer. "I'm guessing the bigger the bubble the bigger the hyper-claims. In between—like when markets are in a steady state—the figures might be accurate. But there'll always be some bezzle."

"Bezzle?" Ken asked Bill, "What's that?"

"It's a word J.K. Galbraith made up. There's always a small but manageable level of misrepresentation or downright lies—bezzle—embezzlement, like static in a signal. It's in times of real crisis that bezzle does a lot of harm."

Sally chipped in, "Like Triple-A trash."

Bill agreed, "Right."

They dropped the issue, so Bob went on, "O.K., we can check off 'Analytical reporting review.' It leaves us with more questions at this point than answers, but it's something you'll have to consider." [SEE NOTE 8-4]

Bob paused for breath. "Now we move on. Next, the 'Communication process.' We did this way back, so you might want to review my hand-out from that class." He paused. This subject was still raw; his casual approach to this had surely been one reason he had been fired. "Communication!" He heard himself almost shouting the word. "You can't get enough of it, and you'll never be able to give enough to please all of the people all of the time! That, by the way, is a mark of these times. It used to be—and this was especially true in investment for insurance—that if a company hired an external manager the message that came with the job was. "'Bye 'bye, see you next quarter!"

Ken commented, "I take it that isn't the case any more." An ironic smile broke out across his customary poker face.

"That's right. The line of communication used to go something like: If we need cash from the portfolio we'll call and give you some warning; or, if we want to send you cash to invest, we'll call and let you know what to expect. Apart from that, an investment manager might operate through quarter after quarter on the principle: If everything's fine, no need to call; if something goes off the rails, the bosses need to know.

"Nowadays you have to make the lines of communication absolutely explicit. Get totally tuned in to the risk appetite of the company, to the spirit of the investment policy."

Bill added, "And get used to a steady flow of panic calls!"

Bob responded fast, "Well, you have to develop a sixth sense for separating routine communications from those 'Drop everything. I'm on the phone to you!' events.

"Any other comments on communications?"

No one spoke. Bob called a break. [SEE NOTE 8-5]

Ten minutes later they were back at work, about to discuss the finer points of 'Stress and sensitivity testing.' Bob had been of two minds about this. It presented the most complex aspect of the evening's agenda. Maybe he should have put it first.

"O.K., folks, 'Stress and sensitivity testing.' Given the present state of the sub-primes, default swap wipe-outs, collapse in the financial markets, and so on, it won't surprise you that stress and sensitivity testing is *huge* right now! Again, I can't impart great wisdom here. My crystal ball is as cloudy as everyone else's. But what I can do is offer a few informed words of warning. Which brings us to 'Black swan events.'

Bill rubbed his hands. "Ah, I've been waiting for this."

"And now you shall have it. In spades! The expression, 'a

black swan,' goes back to eighteenth century Britain, where everybody knew that all swans were white, in the same way we all know the sun comes up in the east and sets in the west. So the figurative phrase 'a black swan' meant something that couldn't happen, an impossibility.

"Then, in April 1770, Lieutenant James Cook landed at Botany Bay, the site of what is now Sydney, Australia. Soon after that, the British established a colonial settlement there, and the settlers discovered to their surprise... Anyone want to guess?"

"Black swans!" Sally answered.

"Hole in one! There they were, flocks of them. Big black birds that weren't supposed to exist. Well, the swans weren't about to switch color, so back in Britain the phrase 'black swan' took on a new meaning. It stopped implying something that was impossible and began referring to something that was highly improbable and most unlikely. The nineteenth century philosopher John Stuart Mill was the first writer to use the term that way so far as I can tell.

"Hence the modern term, 'a black swan event.' Anyone notice something distinctive about that phrase?"

Nobody offered a suggestion.

Bob explained: "It's always written in the singular as if, even now, a black swan event is so unusual it's impossible to have more than one at a time: One *tsunami*, one earthquake, one black swan event."

He paused, ostensibly to check his notes; in fact, to catch his breath. The evening had been long and wearing. "The trouble is—depending on who you believe—the litany of financial messes we are currently going through may represent *several* black swan events taking place more of less simultaneously."

Ken Stiller sat up: "I know what book you've been reading!"

Bob responded, "And I bet you're right, Ken! I've given the reference in my class notes if anyone wants a copy. You may find it useful in setting the general background and scene."

Sally asked, "With all these risk management models, shouldn't acceptable risk lie somewhere near the middle of a normal bell curve?"

Bill added to her comment, "That depends on a board's risk appetite, surely."

Bob explained, "In most cases you would both be right. But the kind of wild macroeconomics we're seeing now *may* be—I repeat, may be—due to a perfect storm-type black swan event."

"If we're reading the same book, the author ascribed World War I and the September 11th attacks to black swan events," Ken suggested. "It's worth reading."

"Here's what the author says. He's, uh, Nassim Taleb, and his book is *The Black Swan: the Impact of the Highly Improbable*. Feel free to add what I leave out, Ken." Bob shifted in his seat and launched into a précis of the book.

"Taleb spoke at the Chartered Financial Analysts meeting in Vancouver in 2007, and this is more or less what he had to say: 'Our current financial models are flawed. You guys—the delegates—are worrying about stuff that's going to happen inside plus or minus two standard deviations. The interesting stuff—what's going down now—is happening out in the tails, in the zones where you might find, in a very rare circumstance, a black swan event.

"In the risk management models that everyone has been using, when the U.S. equities market went down forty percent in 2008, believe it or not *that* was within two standard deviations of equity volatility. Just two to three deviations!

"But the blowout of spreads on the fixed income side—and the problems we've had on fixed income—that was in nobody's model. Nobody's! That's why we saw some of the giants collapse and a lot of them fail. Those incidents were in black swan territory.

"If anyone had really stress-tested these institutions and their 'assets'—I use the term generously—it they had really stress-tested them, they would have found the holes a long time ago.

"But imagine: You're working as a junior analyst at, say, the late-lamented Lehman Brothers. You're accustomed to seeing all sorts of analyses about underwriting these sub-primes and credit default swaps, how they're a sure thing, especially when they're based on mortgage-backed securities."

Bill interjected, "That was high-level bezzle!"

Bob continued, "So, being a bright young analyst, you buy into the paradigm that house prices can only go up. At the very least they'll stay the same. The flow of paper crossing your desk keeps saying: 'Keep it coming! We're going to keep minting money here.'

"Now, imagine you're that junior analyst, and you're saying to yourself: 'Wait a minute. It's possible that house prices can go down, maybe even 20% in a year; and it's possible, given that financial institutions are extending credit to just about everybody, that a lot of these folks won't be able to keep up their mortgages. We might actually see some losses here!'

"If you took your personal assessment to the boss—much of whose remuneration was leveraged against that commercial paper—how long do you think you would keep your job?"

Ken stretched his legs, trying to get a more comfortable position in the classroom chair. Then he ventured his opinion, "A lot of the smaller folks knew or suspected what was going down. They must have done."

Bob agreed, somewhat ruefully. "Oh yeah. You bet they did."

Bill chimed in, "You sound like you speak from personal knowledge, Bob."

Bob nodded assent. "Uh-huh."

"'Uh-huh.' That's all you're going to say?"

Bob summoned up a smile. "Yes. For the moment that's all, Bill." He felt like adding that that was the reason he was teaching night school, but he refrained, drowning the thought and the moment by taking a sip of water.

Ken said quietly, "Since you seem to be sore on this point, would you at least agree that high finance is not a sympathetic place for whistle-blowing?"

"Oh yeah, I can agree to that, especially if it runs counter to a flow of vested interests."

Sally jumped in. "More like a torrent of vested interests in the run-up to our current mess."

"Which takes us," Bill suggested, "from a black swan event to the fact that some of the highest paid brains in finance were playing for an extended period of time at the game called, 'the emperor's new clothes,' until some little boy pointed out: 'These guys are stark naked!'"

"Too darn right," Bob agreed, claiming back the discussion: "I don't want to work this point to death," he concluded, "but my best advice is to emulate that proverbial little boy, read plenty of sources, and if you happen to see a structured security or other 'interesting' security that looks like it's blatantly naked, walk on by!"

Ken couldn't leave it there. "And if you're asked for a professional opinion?"

"Call it like you see it. There's no other way. Look," Bob added, "this is the real rock *versus* a hard place. If you call it like you see it, *you* may be in trouble for going nose to nose against a vested interest. But if you *don't* call it like you see it, a mile down the road our whole society's in trouble. We've seen that happen. Take your pick!"

Nobody spoke. Nobody had to. Bob had made a powerful point. [SEE NOTE 8-6]

Ken Stiller, squirming in his desk and chair set, broke the silence. "There's a coffee shop across the street. Next time we meet, why don't we check in here and then set up in a booth over there?"

Bob called for a show of hands. Everyone agreed. "O.K.," he

said, "I'll print my slides on paper. We'll have a more comfortable evening."

They were pretty drained by now. Bob could see it, but he still had a point to discuss.

"O.K. Last point. This shouldn't take long. 'Changing regulatory or accounting environments.' Let's go over this briefly. The Financial Accounting Standards Board—FAS-BEE to its friends—has taken a lot of heat from Congress lately—aimed at clothing it in shining new clothes, better than the ones we were just talking about!

"It can be tough to come up with fair prices for some bonds, especially ones that aren't traded often. It's especially tough because you have to state the fair value of the bonds you hold on your financials. So FASB will now let you *model* them to come up with fair values.

"And here's an important point—I detect eyes glazing over, but hang in there: You, Mr. or Ms. Portfolio Manager, had better have the intent and the ability to hold onto those bonds, because if they're under water long enough you're going to have to write 'em up as something other than a temporary impairment—and that goes straight to your income statement as a loss, even though it's unrealized."

"Holy cow!" said Bill. "You lost me!"

"O.K. It doesn't get easier. Unless you think you're going to have to sell the bond, then you have to show the loss. If that is *not* the case, if you're going to keep it in the portfolio, don't worry about it. Run it through your shareholders' equity as an unrealized loss, but—here's the good news—it doesn't touch your income statement.

"Now, there's one rule for banks and another for insurance companies. Insurance companies are required to use statutory accounting rules. So we use statutory accounting to figure out how much capital we have, right?"

Silence. Everybody seemed to have had enough.

"There are lots of issues, and we can't get into them here. The point is, monitoring accounting changes is hugely important because it can influence the kind of investment strategy you have." [SEE NOTE 8-7]

Eureka! Suddenly Bob was clutching the desk. The color drained out of his face.

His students looked at each other. Sally asked, "Are you all right, Bob."

"Yes," he told her. "I'm fine, thanks." But what he was thinking was: 'This was likely why I was fired!'

He had made one too many decisions that had improved the portfolio—but by writing down the stated income it had also chopped senior management's fees. Nobody had complained about his performance when times were fat, but when they turned down… He wanted to be sick.

"Hey," he said, surveying the weary faces, "let's call it a night. See you next week. We'll meet here and go across the street."

CHAPTER 8 NOTES

Bob's certainty of what constitutes performance monitoring is to be admired. However....

NOTE 8-1

Bob's certainty of what constitutes performance monitoring is to be admired. However, in the increasingly volatile and changing world of finance and financial markets, Bob's list becomes—just a good start!

None of the fancy risk management models in the world contemplated the liquidity and credit meltdowns of 2008 in the fixed-income markets, along with the subsequent fallout. And that means that portfolio monitoring has a certain creative element in it. What might occur that we are not contemplating? How should we monitor for such an event? How would we react in such a situation? These are just some of the questions that must be asked when developing a process for portfolio monitoring.

But, Bob's class must start at the basics they must never ignore, so let's rejoin them.

NOTE 8-2

It is indeed easy to sail close to the wind for some investment managers. This goes back to earlier comments about investment manager style. All managers will do their best to outperform the benchmark within the parameters of the policy. But some managers will stretch to the limits the policy in doing so.

For example, we remember one manager who utilized TBA securities tied to mortgages plus Treasury bills in order to replicate the performance of an investment in a standard mortgage-backed security (MBS). TBAs are basically short term commitments to purchase a future pool of mortgages within certain specifications. From a risk management standpoint, the manager's approach seemed reasonable provided the overall exposure was equal to the investment in a similar MBS. However, the company's investment policy had specifically not allowed investment in derivatives (usually defined as an instrument whose change in value is tied to the change in value of another reference instrument or investment).

'Are TBAs derivatives?' became the question. The insurer said something like, 'If it looks like a duck and quacks like a duck...' it must be a derivative. And the manager said, 'We're simply investing in a more efficient manner and providing the same exposure as an MBS at lower cost—and these MBSs are perfectly O.K. under the policy.' Who won this battle? Unsurprisingly, the company's view prevailed (it is their assets, after all), and the manager had to change its ways.

NOTE 8-2

More importantly, the issue here was not one of interpretation but of communication. Should the manager have realized that they were sailing too close to the wind? Of course. Was the manager maintained on this account despite superior performance versus the benchmark? Of course not. Finding the right manager is about more than performance when it comes to insurer assets.

NOTE 8-3

Now consider the example of the manager who knew the insurer was in the process of an investment manager search. The company was unsure if they would make a change—they had not done so for about a decade and the incumbent was doing alright over the long haul, but not so well over the short term.

Realizing that they needed to bring up their performance in the short term, and that this was their Achilles' heel in the selection process, the manager found a course of action that could 'goose' their returns. They loaded up on high yield debt (mostly BB, one level below investment grade) to the maximum allowed by the policy, hoping that markets would recover over the next quarter or so and allow them to look better in the eyes of the selection committee. This 'Hail Mary' attempt at improving performance, though, backfired miserably, pulling the company's portfolio deeper into poor performance.

Should the policy have been changed in contemplation of this possible move by the manager? Assuming a solid strategic asset allocation was devised, there really should not be a need to change the policy.

Or, should the manager have been told to 'freeze' all trades while the search was on? Probably not, as the manager was not told it would be fired, only that they were included in the overall evaluation of investment managers. Why tie their hands when they had developed some level of trust over years of operation?

NOTE 8-3

So, what probably should have been done? Better portfolio monitoring. Too often companies review the portfolio in detail only at quarter end. A solid, ongoing portfolio monitoring process would reveal some unusually active purchases of high yield bonds, and cause a spotlight to be put on this rather unusual behavior. That is one way to make certain that the policy design is working in practice.

Undoubtedly Bob fully realizes this, but he has a lot of topics to cover today for a very focused student body.

NOTE 8-4

Let's take the example of credit ratings as noted by the cynical Ken. Can one truly trust the rating agencies now? More importantly: What should we use to get our arms around credit risk?

There is, of course, a possibility that the credit rating agencies' business model will be changed either due to market and/or governmental pressures. Meanwhile, the largest agencies churn out ratings while collecting fees from the entities they rate, a built-in conflict of interest.

However, investment policy after investment policy speaks of the requirement of a 'minimum average credit rating' of 'X' for the portfolio in an effort to maintain credit risk at some level of minimum quality. What can be done to better manage credit risk?

First, recalculate the portfolio's average credit rating. Let's consider that the 'average credit rating' calculated by virtually every investment manager and every investment portfolio analysis program assumes that credit risk deteriorates on a linear basis as one goes down the credit risk spectrum. Thus, for example, a AAA rated bond is given a '1', AA a '2', A a '3', BBB a '4' and so forth and then everything is weighted by, for example, market value and an average is determined.

NOTE 8-4

However, the reality is that credit risk does not increase in a linear fashion as one moves down the ratings path. Instead, it increases closer to an exponential rather then a linear function. Thus, one must re-weight bonds in the portfolio based upon the expected default rate for that specific credit rating. These statistics are freely available from the rating agencies themselves, so there should be little in the way of hurdles to performing this calculation.

Yet, investment managers continue to churn out analytic reports using the linear estimation of credit risk. How wrong could they be? In practice, about one to three 'clicks' (where a 'click' is, for example, the difference between an AA- and an A+ portfolio) worse than the linear method.

Second, manager reports showing credit rating agency ratings must be supplemented by the internal ratings of the investment manager. In today's increasingly challenging financial markets, this is where many companies that do not use external managers and do not have deep credit-analytic staffs seem to be missing the boat. In today's environment, we think the credit rating is a suggestion of credit risk, but the manager's opinion (assuming a strong and deep analytical approach) should be worth a lot more in determining what the 'true' credit risk may be.

NOTE 8-4

The important issue here is that all of the major credit rating agencies are paid by the issuer for their ratings. That is akin to the movie studios paying your favorite movie critics for a positive review. One would be skeptical of such a relationship when researching what movie to watch, so why wouldn't one be even more skeptical when one's investment portfolio is involved? Thus, an investment manager with superior and deep credit skills is vital to a successful investment process.

Investment managers take various and sometimes creative approaches to providing and analyzing credit risk. You should be certain that your company is 100% comfortable with the approach and the analysis. If not, please see Chapter 7 and review investment management, responsibility and evaluation.

NOTE 8-5

Like Bob, we stress that a CIO, such as he had been, must establish and enforce a firm communications policy with his investment manager. The key is to develop a communications protocol and understand what is expected of the manager and the company in the relationship.

Importantly, this should be reviewed periodically as well. A given communications protocol that might have served the company well in quieter times might not be appropriate in every situation.

NOTE 8-6

The rule of thumb in today's financial markets?

Stress test, stress test and then stress test some more. It is both careless and perilous to take the results of any risk management, asset/liability management or DFA model and use the results as the major basis of your financial decisions. Thus, all of these models must also be stress-tested for potentially unique and unusual situations. The difficulty comes in defining the stress scenarios and in how to use those stress tests.

Should we manage to these stress scenarios occurring? If we do, we will undoubtedly produce poorer financial results in most situations, but look rather foresighted should those stress scenarios occur. Thus, it is very important to understand the implications behind the stress tests, their likelihood and if the insurer is comfortable in forgoing performance, to some degree in most situations, while being prepared for that stressed scenario.

As we have seen in recent history, stress situations have subsequently evoked governmental activity. And, it is here that finance quickly turns from mathematics and economic/financial relationships to looking more like sociology—the study of human social structure and activity. To that, with increasing government involvement in the economy, we would add that a careful knowledge of political science is also a good idea.

NOTE 8-6

Thus, a good deal of creativity plus deep financial experience and knowledge is a prerequisite for developing and using stress tests. And questioning the results based upon non-financial factors found in the realm of sociology and political science can make the results and decision-making richer.

NOTE 8-7

It seems that the 'tail' of accounting truly 'wags the dog' of investment decisions—and that's a growing trend. The importance of understanding an investment strategy or decision in light of tax, statutory, generally accepted accounting principals as well as other metrics has gained in importance.

Thus, it is important to understand not only the current state of accounting and regulatory affairs as they relate to investments, but also where things are headed. That, in turn, may determine how accounting and regulatory issues might hinder economic decisions made by investment professionals.

We will discuss that most important of accounting issues, Other Than Temporary Impairment (OTTI), in the next chapter. However, beyond OTTI, issues such as what is the fair value of a security and how gains/losses are reflected under the various accounting rubrics are most important in implementing and monitoring a successful investment process for an insurer.

9

PERFORMANCE MEASUREMENT

A NOT SO SIMPLE TASK

Sitting quietly on his bench, Bob called to Molly, "I guess the key to performance measurement means that an insurance company really has tough decisions to make." The dog's expanding leash reeled in and out as she rushed around busily, hunting for scents. The leash in Bob's hand sounded like a fly-fishing reel. Boyhood thoughts came rushing back: O, if there were only a river ahead of him instead of a narrow strip of blacktop through a newish development!

"It's tougher than choosing: 'Which color of Kibble is it?' Moll." He had reached into his pocket and produced two small pellets of the compressed dog food, one nearly black, the other reddish-brown. Molly had already scoffed the black one. "No more for you until you've heard the lesson. Listen carefully!"

There was no better place to rehearse class notes than out in the open, with a more or less obliging audience of one. Bob returned the second piece of Kibble to his pocket, then absent-mindedly scratched Molly between her ears. She returned the favor, closing dark eyes and extending her tongue, slobbering on Bob's hand.

"Yuck! You are a messy puppy!"

This pleased her immensely. She hopped onto the park bench beside him before jumping down again, her front paws scratching the grass. It was her way of saying it was time to get lost in the bushes and toss around newly fallen leaves.

"Not so fast, lady! You, Molly, are the Chief Investment Officer of a large insurance company, and you have an important decision to make: To what extent are you going to concentrate on investment income, or on yield? And to what extent are those two factors going to focus on total return?"

Molly barked, impatiently, and looked towards the inviting bush.

"First question, Moll. I bet you can't tell me the difference between yield and return."

Molly growled softly, imagining dangerous things in the thicket of green.

"Yield is the measure of the income you get from an asset. It does not take into account any changes in the market value of that asset, so it doesn't include capital gains or losses."

The dog looked at her master pityingly, then cocked her head to one side, as if that might help her improve her perspective on a dull fellow.

"Take a fixed income bond, Molly. The yield of a bond is its yield to maturity. It's not exactly the same as coupon payments from an accounting perspective, but it's pretty close. If you buy a bond at a premium it may have a coupon of 5%, but your yield is maybe 4.5%. So you get to accrue 4.5% of income on your balance sheet, namely your income statement. That's the yield part."

Molly was panting, poised to take off, a veritable jackrabbit on short, stumpy legs.

"Sit, Moll! Good girl. Stay!" [SEE NOTE 9-1]

Bob had tried working up his notes with Sue, but she had no head for figures and didn't pretend to. His wife had a degree in constitutional history, and had taught business administration courses at a community college before they married. At the moment it looked as though she might go back to teaching again.

Bob took in the woods bordering the small park, the quiet road through the unfinished development, and the leaden sky. Soon the trees would be bare. Essentially an introvert, he was often content to be alone. If it were true that he was unemployed, it was also true that his personal philosophy was essentially Stoic—his mechanism for coping with adversity was to imagine that things could be worse. Much worse. Bob sat on the bench, considering his restless dog and counting his many blessings.

"O.K., Molly, we'll move out soon." At the sound of her name she pricked up her ears, then deflated them again, as if to say: You're kidding me, right?

"We talked about income and yield in the world of bonds, kiddo. On the other hand, in the world of equities your yield is usually the dividend," Bob instructed her. "Dividends are usually a tiny part of your equity gains or losses. In equities the change in the value of your stock typically swamps the income component from a dividend.

"Fetch, Moll!" Bob threw a Kibble in a safe direction, away from the road. The leash shrieked as she ran, tugging its reel.

"So," he addressed her over his shoulder, "in the world of statutory accounting for U.S. insurers, you take the changing value and it runs right through your surplus."

Molly couldn't find the Kibble in the grass. She started digging in pure frustration. Bob pulled another piece from his pocket and clicked his tongue. She came rushing back.

"If you sell an equity, the figures carry through your profit and loss statement. Or in your case, Moll, right through your gut."

Molly gobbled the treat and sat back, waiting for another.

There wasn't one.

"Well might you look disappointed," Bob told her. "Because now there's another hook. If a stock or bond tanks far enough and long enough, then you have the possibility of being stuck with an 'other than temporary impairment'—that's OTTI—which truly is a four letter word. You'll probably have to write it down on your profit and loss. Then the question becomes: is this going to hurt your earnings, your ability to pay dividends, or—heaven help us!—wash out your incentive compensation? Bob voiced the phrase with a trace of bitterness mixed with disdain. For senior management, executive comp. might depend on current earnings. [SEE NOTE 9-2]

"So that's the difference between yield and total return. Yield is often considered in the context, 'What's the yield on the portfolio?' It's sort of just investment income, whereas total return means the total economic value of what's going on in the portfolio."

A short pause ensued. Dog and man considered each other.

"Come on, Molly!" Bob stood up. "Let's take a hike on your adventure trail."

Small animals had beaten a narrow path through the woods at this point. The path was even visible where it emerged into the grass of the park. "Molly, when we get to the place you like where the path forks, we'll be confronting a wonderful example of risk adjustment. Which way lies promise; which way threat?"

They entered the gloom of the woods, the dog pulling ahead, the man recalling the days of toting a full pack and an M16 on exercises over craggy basalt outcrops in the woods around West Point.

Molly skirted a tall, beautiful fern growing in the path. Animals had walked around it on both sides, leaving the fern untouched and undamaged. Bob followed the dog.

"Managers typically show total return numbers, and they'll always compare the figure to that total return number we talked about earlier, Moll. So, they'll know if we did better or worse—and the next step is to risk-adjust the numbers to see if, on a risk-adjusted basis, the portfolio manager added value, or not! And the risk that's adjusted..."

Bob tripped on a root, *thump*, almost running over Molly before he recovered himself.

"...The risk that's adjusted, usually due to the volatility of the returns... Where was I? The more you go down the total return path, the more you can apply the old CFA-type literature that says: now we'll do a Sharpe Ratio, and we're going to do an information ratio, and we can trot out numbers from unconstrained accounts, where folks don't have to worry about realized gains and losses..."

Molly stopped, ostensibly to check out an animal burrow, more likely to save face. She had to catch her breath. She had been pulling so hard on the leash she was throttling herself.

"Very clever, the Sharpe Ratio, and dead simple," Bob told her. "It tells you how much extra return you are receiving in exchange for the increased volatility you have to put up with for holding a riskier asset.

"Whatever that means," he mused, "at a time when every piece of commercial paper on a desk was rated Triple-A!"

They were approaching the far side of the little wood. The trees filtered sounds of children playing on a lawn ahead of them. More immediately, branches soughed above them and their steps kicked up the rustle of fallen leaves. [SEE NOTE 9-3]

"Those sorts of measurements tell us: Where our portfolio was, and our manager, in terms of total return at different time periods with respect to these different risk measures. Trouble is, Molly, these measures are all unconstrained. To a degree we're comparing apples and oranges. We're comparing our insurance portfolios with folks who can trade and get in and out of sectors as fast as they want. But the poor schlep who's managing investments for an insurance company has to consider: O my, if

I do X, what's that do to my investment income? And if I do Y, I might have to take a loss, and my realized loss is going to worm its darned way right through my P and L, and I can't do that because the chief investment officer says to limit realized losses to—well, you know how it is!"

Molly did indeed know. She sat up, begging, and whined.

"No more bonuses, Moll, not till we get home to Sue."

Bob propped his back against the trunk of a spruce. Ever since his days as a cadet he had felt a sort of *Last of the Mohicans* sense of presence in woods. He whispered to the dog, as if they were spying on Fort Ticonderoga: "See, the trouble is, those sorts of comparisons are spurious, but they're comparisons some folks like to make."

Molly was sniffing around a tree trunk. Something held her attention, fascinated.

Bob chipped in, "There's comfort in data that reinforces one's prejudice, don't you find, no matter it may be flawed or dead wrong!"

The dog sneezed.

"Shh, Moll. Hush! The point I'm making is: It's the insurance company's choice. Most of 'em look at both yield and return, but to what extend do they focus on yield *versus* total return?"

The sun had disappeared among the trees, its disk just visible above the horizon, among the trunks. Time to head home.

"Come on, Moll. Finish your business and let me clean up. Then we'll go see Sue. But first I have to make one point: Most domestic insurers look more to yield than to total return because they are concerned with the bottom line. Their attitude is: I want to make sure I'm getting competitive yield adjusted for risk. You gotta ask yourself: Here's your portfolio of corporate bonds. Some of them are going to go bad. How do I adjust for that? Insurers need insurance, too. You have to set up a reserve.

"Hey, Moll, don't pee on that fern! Get your ass over here.

That's better: That little tree could use the fertilizer."

Bob turned and headed back along the narrow track, now almost invisible in the waning light. Molly snuffled along behind.

"The question is, Moll, from an insurer's point of view, which way is the wind gonna blow?" [SEE NOTE 9-4]

"The point is, Bob, you'd better know why you were fired!" Jeremy Libertz grabbed up his knight with a very large hand and plopped it down, displacing one of Bob's pawns. Then he took the piece off the board and drank a shot of soda. "I mean, I'm talking game theory here. It's not important to know why it was convenient for those S.O.Bs to ditch you. That's not what I'm saying. What I mean is: you better know your own weak points and work on them so you can ace an interview, and then a job. Virtual reality beats real time waffle. The real gamer wins."

"O.K., so where do I begin?"

"You did already. You 'fessed up to communications, or lack of it. Start there and build. You heard of *kaizen*?"

"What's that?"

"From the mists of old Japan—it's the practice of improving or repairing, taking baby steps, one at a time. Modern engineers use it like attaining six sigma enlightenment in manufacturing. More to the point, *kaizen* has become a psychologists' buzzword, it's a tool to fix folks who got themselves dysfunctional in some respect. It's psychotherapy with a practical outcome. Not that I'm implying…"

"Point taken, Jem."

"The first thing you need to know is what to improve. Then you can write a job app. and ace an interview with perfect certainty that you're the real thing. You've got the numbers, man. Show 'em your stats!"

"And I've got no faults at all! Sheer genius," Bob added, laconically.

"Right!" returned Jem. "You're a rare case of brains beating bullshit, my man." Jem held up his glass of soda and squinted through it. "Let me look into my crystal ball and tell you, Bob Short, based on what we know, why Greening fired you. And by the way, first out of the gate, I would expand your faulty communication practices to take in the board of directors as well as line management."

Bob agreed. "You'd be right there. As far as I was concerned, they were distant suits in a far-off land."

"Down their own rabbit holes, yes, but they knew the whats and whys behind their bonus checks. You know your trouble, Bob? You're no goddamn politician. You've got your nose to the grindstone, giving your all to the company. Eyes down and get on with the job. Trouble is, that's not the kind of guy who rules the world. I bet you didn't even know the names of those chumps on the board, did you?"

"I made presentations to them every month. Beyond that…"

"Beyond that you gave them no reasons to love you."

"They did very well out of my portfolio decisions in the good times."

"Yeah, I bet you did them proud. But that was history. When good times go bad, 'vested interest' memory kicks in hard!"

"What's that?"

"About six seconds—the short term memory of a goldfish."

"Hey, Jem, some of those people didn't know nuts about the operation."

Jeremy retorted, "It doesn't matter. Some honcho put them there. They might have been dumb to the day by day, but not stupid."

The men were still in the opening stages of their game of chess, but now the board and the pieces went largely abandoned. It was Bob's future they were playing for.

"Here's a scenario—and you can make a Greek tragedy of this, if you will!" Jem smiled across the table. "Once upon a time there was a chief investment officer who was told his performance would be measured on a total return relative to a benchmark, and that his incentive compensation would be based on that."

Bob nodded.

"Meanwhile, everyone participated in a general bonus pool based on net income. So when things were going great on the realized gain side, our CIO was a hero. His performance versus the benchmark was O.K., too, so he got a bit of a bonus. Everyone else, especially the top guns, got a ton of bonus cash. Our man was adorned with laurel wreaths. Then things turned sour and the new world wasn't nice no more.

"Now our man reports to his bosses and the board: 'Hey, we lost $20 million in OTTIs, but we beat our benchmark by fifty basis points.' Well, the board finds this enticing as bad fish. They're like: 'You took twenty mill in losses!'

" 'That's not me,' says our babe in Wonderland. 'That's the accountants. The markets are tough and they have to follow accounting rules.'

"All of a sudden, everyone from the janitor up gets a bonus of zip. Where does that take us, Bob?"

"Out the door, I guess."

"Yeah, but not necessarily. First, it gets us back to communication. People can accept bad news if you set 'em up for it. And the way things were, you had time to do that. The whole world was tanking, for Pete's sake."

Bob looked glum, but he had no excuses. "That's true," he agreed.

Jem leaned forward, as if to confide. "Here, my son, let me tell you a parable."

Bob took a gulp of weak scotch and waited for the inevitable.

Jem began, "Maybe our man suddenly fell out of love with a bond. So he sold it and he got eighty cents on the dollar. That's a big loss. But the value of that bond kept dropping. So a month later he walked into the boss's office and said, 'Phew, good thing

I got out of that bond when I did. It's only worth forty cents on the dollar now.'

"But his boss is telling himself, 'Hey, you creep, my bonus went south with your 80-cent sale. I don't give a toss that you sold for a good fire-sale price and saved the company a pile of cash.' That's what the boss is thinking."

"That's a bit cynical, Jem."

"Nah, that stuff is happening out there all the time. There's real fear in the air. The old Chinese classic, the *Tao Te Ching*, has a great line: 'A man is wealthy who knows when he has enough.' Think about that for a heartbeat or two!

"Listen, Bob," Jem continued, "half the clowns in investment banking don't have a cut-off switch on greed. I used to let people beat up on me from time to time, and I'd walk away smiling, 'cause I got peace of mind. The other guys? Let 'em be rich and die young."

The room fell silent. Only now did the slow drip from a distant kitchen tap make itself heard.

Jem was on a verbal roll. He went on, "Let's come down to earth and talk about you. From Greening's perspective, and maybe the board's, they need a new incentive plan, a new way of looking at performance and rating it—and, too bad for you, Bob—they may have figured out they needed a new guy to approach things differently."

"By 'new' you mean a team player who understands where everybody's bonuses come from—and screw the company."

"Hey, Bob, you look genuinely surprised."

"Too true, Jem. Too true."

"You spent too long in officer-and-gentleman school. Me, I came up the hard way—with sharp elbows. Hey, cheer up, Bob. Better you learn too late than not at all!"

For the sake of form and the school's regulations, Bob and his students checked into their classroom at the community college, then turned off the lights and crossed the road to a coffee shop, where they took places at a round table and spread out their notes.

"This being our last class, I thought I'd bring you up to date on the real world out there," Bob told his group. "I had a good job doing what you hope to be doing soon, based on the practice I'm describing here—until I got fired!"

Sitting across from Bob, Bill Hanna didn't miss a beat. "I gotta tell you, we wondered: Why else would a high-flyer with all the answers be teaching night-school?"

"A lot of successful people teach night-school, Bill. And I was never a high-flyer. Just ex-Army with a head for numbers and precision—too much precision, maybe."

"You can never get enough precision!" Ken Stiller, a deputy controller for a department of state government, seemed shocked. To say the least, Ken had a marked reserve. Perhaps 'stiff personality' described him better. Bob noticed he had given up wearing a tie to class, but Ken was still brittle. What was he doing here? Surely he would never quit a senior government job in return for uncertain prospects as an investment officer. Or maybe his prospects weren't that certain. Government was laying off, too.

Bob told him, "So far I've kept this course on an absolute level, outlining the pure—and I mean pure—function of what you have to do to keep a *portfolio* on track. But what do you have to do to keep your *career* on track? Office politics gets in the way. So now, folks, I'll tell you my tale!"

"You mean there's a dark side to being an investment officer?" Sally Prentice was sitting to Bob's right, her head turned slightly away as she spoke. He sensed a note of anxiety in her voice, rather than irony, her normally confident tone ill at ease. A single mother, perhaps Sally had been hoping for a job with more certainty in uncertain times. Bob was sorry if he had disappointed or misled her. Maybe if he gave this course again he would mix the office politics with the practical guide up front.

He let down Sally gently. "Practically by definition we're talking about being employed by large organizations, and I don't know of one that exists without internal feuds and strife. At least I can tell you what to look out for."

Bob sipped his coffee, then put his cup on his notes. "I was hired on the basis that I would be measured on a total return relative to a benchmark, and that my incentive compensation would be based on that. Fair enough. Meanwhile, everybody had a slice in the general bonus pool based on net income. Of course that included any realized gains and losses. So when things were going great on the realized gain side, I was a hero.

"Then came the turnaround. We lost $20 million in OTTI on bonds… Who can tell me what that stands for?"

Ken and Sally pounced, almost in unison, "Other than temporarily impaired."

"Permanently screwed!" added Bill.

"Right on both counts," Bob agreed, ruefully. "Well, there were no bonuses. Fact is, if I hadn't sold those bonds right then and there we would have lost more, but the board, or whoever!—I don't know who put out the contract on me—didn't seem to think that was much of an excuse."

"So you were out," said Bill.

"So I was out. Boy, was I naïve. I went into a meeting with the message: 'I know the market's tough, guys, but look at this. We beat our benchmark by fifty basis points.' Meaning, of course, that I beat the benchmark they had set me for my incentive comp.—but the loss wiped out their bonuses.

"I was focused on total return with the idea that as long as I produced enough investment income, I was keeping the company happy."

"Is that what they told you specifically, why you were fired?" Sally asked.

"No. Not specifically. I've had to piece the bits together

with help from wiser friends. Look, everything else was *kosher*. I invested according to policy. We were compliant all the way.

"I suspect my boss was told in no uncertain terms: 'Get rid of Short and find us someone who understands the game.'"

"Even if I had a mind to be cynical," Ken was stirring his latte like an automaton, "I'd say your previous employers need more than bonuses. They need a new perspective and a new incentive plan, one designed for tough times."

"And you, of course, need a new job," Bill added thoughtfully.

"Yeah!" Bob was emphatic. "I'm working on that."

Ken still stirred his cup, still mused on the sudden end to 'normal' times. "I guess most of us thought the worst case was going to be equity markets dropping by forty percent. That's, what, two or three standard deviations. Maybe a black swan event. But no one expected the bond markets to blow out like they did."

"It's like, you don't plan for a *tsunami* in Kansas," added Bill.

Someone mumbled, "That's right."

Bob steered the discussion back on course. "Maybe we'd better say something about remuneration for performance. Whether it's adjusted based on return or on yield, it should be looked at net of fees, and net of any external manager fees. And—before and after tax. Where this goes critical is where the portfolio is making substantial gains, because you're losing 34 cents on the dollar on your gains."

"It'll be a year or two before we get there again," said Sally.

"If ever," Bill added, gloomily.

Bob ploughed on: "Of course, any measurement of performance needs 'performance attribution.' That sets out the whys behind your performance. It asks: Why did you, or somebody else, under- or over-perform against a total return benchmark?

"In the world of fixed income, you typically look at it like: "Did you perform well because of changes in interest rates including changes in the yield curve? Was it because you happened to be in the right sector, overweight in corporates, or underweight in mortgage backed securities—whatever the case might be?

"Never forget performance attribution. It's important. It gives the whys behind performance." Bob heard and felt himself running out of steam. Getting another coffee was not the answer. Time to wrap up. "For example, is one of your managers dithering while the market moves, and holding maybe 25% of your money in cash? If he's in this market your money is sitting there earning 20 basis points while you're paying the guy a fee of 40. That's nuts! That's why performance measurement matters. You're looking at your overall portfolio inside and out, from all sorts of standpoints. [SEE NOTE 9-5]

"The key message you take away tonight is: Performance measurement is more than crunching numbers; it's not just a clerical task. As a manager you need to give it the full weight of your expertise.

"It's asking the whys behind that maze of decisions, stalls and compromises you and the others had to take, and figuring out what's most important, return versus yield, and to what extent."

Bob had pretty much run out of words.

Bill Hanna noticed immediately: "Is that it?"

"I guess it is," Bob acknowledged. "That's a wrap."

Bill went on, "We're cast out on a wild sea, to sink or to swim!"

Even Ken Stiller managed a smile.

"Me, too," Bob reminded them. "As for you three, you seem to have done well this far. No reason why you shouldn't win out in the end."

The party broke up, people exchanged business cards, and

they headed for the parking lot. Bob waited while they drove away, acknowledging each in turn. Whatever else giving this course had done for him, it left him with a sense of achievement and satisfaction.

CHAPTER NOTES

If only Bob had as much luck getting his Board and senior management team . . . .

NOTE 9-1

If only Bob had as much luck getting his Board and senior management team to listen up as he had with Molly. The dog listens carefully to the difference between yield and total return, but too many Boards and senior management teams simply focus on one or the other, as it pleases them, without settling on exactly which is more important, to what degree and why.

Yield provides a measure of investment income, so it is invaluable in seeing how much the investment portfolio contributes to the company's bottom line. From an accounting perspective, it is difficult to beat yield as a measure of success. However, as you have probably realized by now, there are exceptions to the rule. Higher yields come with higher risks and the question one must always ask about the yield on a portfolio is, "Does it accurately include the amount of risk in the portfolio?" Or, put more plainly, "Are we getting paid for the risk we are taking?"

Some of the risks that should be considered include credit risk, interest rate risk and liquidity risk. But, there are other risks that may be hiding in the portfolio. Perhaps the best example of a hidden risk is the accuracy of the credit ratings of the bonds in the portfolio. As long as rating agencies are being paid by the issuers to rate bonds, there is the potential for severe conflicts of interest and the probability of the agencies' rating being skewed by the income potential from the issuer. One would hope this model will change in the future,

NOTE 9-1

but as long as the rating agencies are profit maximizing enterprises with revenue from issuers, this risk must be considered. But how can one do so?

Start by considering that the rating agency may be wrong. Give the rating a 'haircut' – one or more rating clicks (a movement say from A to A- would be one 'click') and then reconsider the portfolio's overall credit risk profile. That is just one way to reconsider credit risk.

Another way is to estimate the default function and loss given default function of a given portfolio. By utilizing the actual (or 'haircut') ratings, one can estimate the likelihood of default and, subsequently, loss given default, for each of the securities in the bond portfolio. These statistics are freely available from the rating agencies in studies they publish. From this, one can determine the expected credit loss from any given portfolio of bonds. Of course, this can result in a 'credit risk' charge to reduce the yield one expects to receive on the portfolio. And, this should generally correlate with a 'normalized' impact on the income statement, which reflects investment income as well as any realized losses, including Other Than Temporarily Impaired securities.

However, this would be a point estimate of loss and, as we all know, that is merely the most likely occurrence. Another way of viewing estimated loss on a portfolio is by reviewing the default or loss given

NOTE 9-1

default function, which utilizes stochastics (a fancy word for random simulations) to determine what the probability of a given loss is over a given time horizon. This, of course, is quite a bit more complicated than the point estimate of default, but it can provide an idea of a reasonable 'worst' case loss from credit risk in the portfolio.

But, this digresses from the discussion of yield versus total return. Where yield definitely directly impacts the income statement, total return may or may not. And, here is where we must digress once again to consider the type of accounting being discussed.

Insurance companies typically file three types of financial statements, each following a slightly different accounting convention: GAAP (Generally Accepted Accounting Principles, as promulgated primarily by the FASB and the SEC), STAT (Statutory Accounting Principles, as promulgated by the NAIC – National Association of Insurance Commissioners and their local state insurance department), and TAX (Accounting principles as required by the Internal Revenue Service).

Most insurers make financial decisions based upon either GAAP or STAT since these are used as the typical yardsticks of financial success, while TAX accounting is usually considered a by-product of one or the other accounting conventions. In fact, if you ask an insurer CFO they usually have a very good idea of which method, GAAP or STAT, is more important. In some cases, they will even virtually ignore one because

NOTE 9-1

of the importance of the others. In some other cases, the company may not file a GAAP statement because it is not legally required. And, in just a few other cases, state regulations have made STAT quite identical to GAAP statements.

Alas, currently GAAP accounting provides an option for companies to vary the way they present and account for investments. Without getting into too much detail, GAAP usually allows companies to account for changes in unrealized gains and losses on investments in one of three basic ways: (1) all unrealized gains and losses flow through the income statement and are reflected in the net income of the company, (2) all unrealized gains and losses are reflected in something called 'Other Comprehensive Income', doesn't directly impact reported net income, but does impact shareholders' equity (also known as net worth) of the company, or (3) some combination of (1) and (2) depending upon how the investment is characterized on the balance sheet.

For STAT accounting, all fixed income instruments are held at amortized cost (book value) and nearly all unrealized gains and losses are not reflected on the income statement and balance sheet, with an exception for bonds that are below investment grade effectively having their unrealized loss run through the income statement. (This varies for life/health versus property/casualty companies, but the general concept of below investment grade bonds usually finding

NOTE 9-1

their gain/loss through the income statement is generally the same for both types of companies.) For investments in unaffiliated equities, any unrealized gains and losses impact surplus (STAT accounting's name for net worth).

For both GAAP and STAT, realized gains and losses are reflected in the income statement. And Other Than Temporary Impaired (OTTI) losses are also reflected on the income statement.

As you can tell, an insurer's desire to measure total return will be heavily influenced by GAAP or STAT importance, as well as the accounting options chosen under GAAP.

But, there can be no denying that total return (investment income plus or minus realized and unrealized losses) provides a better view of the economic value provided by an investment over a given period of time. Meanwhile, yield provides a view of the investment income contribution only – and before an assessment of risks. Of course, those risks may or may not be accurately captured in the market value. Thus, total return may not accurately capture the imbedded (hidden) risk in the portfolio either.

Most insurers, realizing the importance of both measures in assessing performance, review both yield and total return to varying degrees, based upon how they measure financial success.

NOTE 9-1

As you can tell, this is not a discussion that Molly would sit still for and, alas, some senior management teams and Board members might follow suit. However, it is an important discussion that is vital to making certain everyone knows how the relative success or failure of the investment process can initially be measured.

NOTE 9-2

Bob's dislike for OTTI is shared by many within the insurance industry. The reason for OTTI is simple, though the definition is not. The accounting profession realized that not writing down investments or other assets when the ultimate realization of the value shown on the balance sheet was in question was a serious and growing problem. If the financial statements don't accurately state values, what value could the accountant's opinion about following 'generally accepted accounting principles' have? And if that opinion had questionable value, the auditor's role would be open to serious question. So, from the accountant's stand point, OTTI is one answer to a real and present threat.

However, accountants did not major in English, as one can tell by their tagging impairments that are not permanent, per accounting literature, as 'other than temporarily impaired'. You see, the accountants already had something called 'temporary impairments' in their guidance and those were not treated very conservatively at all. So, they had to come up with something that wasn't 'permanent' but also wasn't 'temporary'. That is like calling something that isn't 'heavy' or 'light' – polar opposites – 'other than heavy'. No one in their right mind would understand what you are saying. And, indeed, that has been the result, so far, of the implementation of 'Other Than Temporary Impairment.'

NOTE 9-2

Rules differ a bit depending upon whether GAAP or STAT is being presented. However, the end result is effectively the same for both: OTTI becomes a charge to income.

Importantly, those rules are squishy enough that there is significant variation in application depending upon the company, accounting firm and even the office of the accounting firm.

There are insurers who write down the value of US Treasuries as OTTI because they have fallen sufficiently below book value (usually about 20% as a rule of thumb) for a given period (a rule of thumb of six consecutive months), despite the fact that the fall in value has absolutely nothing to do with credit related losses. For these firms, the fact that they do not have the intent to hold the security until maturity (even though they may have the required ability to hold) means they must recognize a loss today because, if not, it will probably be recognized in the future before it fully recovers to book value.

On the other end of the spectrum are insurers who fight the implication that any bond they hold may be subject to OTTI, despite evidence of material price deterioration. And, in some cases, those insurers are correct. According to FASB guidance, the price used to determine deterioration may be vastly understated due to liquidity issues in the market that have nothing to do with the specific bond being reviewed.

NOTE 9-2

In such a case, this must be considered in determining a more reasonable price and that should be used in determining whether a bond is OTTI.

So, OTTI is a key issue whether considering yield or total return as a measure of performance. In fact, it transcends both of them to some degree, while being another measure of performance in itself, despite its incredibly arbitrary nature.

NOTE 9-3

Bob has mentioned the Sharpe ratio, but there are other measures of risk adjustment that might be considered in the total return world.

The Sharpe ratio tells us how much return in excess of the 'risk free' return we received per unit of risk (volatility calculated as standard deviation of returns). An interesting and important concept, but one that lumps all risks together and defines risk as standard deviation (both very good and very bad results).

Another risk measure typically used is the Information ratio, which uses the same calculation as the Sharpe ratio with one substitution. Instead of return in excess of the 'risk free' return, we look at return in excess of the benchmark. Thus, the Information ratio tells us how much return over or under the benchmark was achieved, adjusted for risk (once again, risk is defined as standard deviation).

Because standard deviation equally considers very good and very bad results, some insurers will modify the Sharpe and Information ratios by using downside risk instead of overall risk, where downside risk is defined as the standard deviation of 'bad' returns (below the benchmark or below risk free returns).

There are many, many more ways of risk adjusting total return and I think that goes back to the old story about the man who asked the investment consultant what time it was. The consultant

NOTE 9-3

then told him, in intricate detail, how the watch was made.

Seriously, these risk adjusted measures can be overdone and, in and of themselves, they tell us very little. Only by asking questions of your investment manager as well as a non-watch-making consultant, and having an open discussion, can these risk adjusted measures truly shed light on performance.

But, as Bob will tell us, even these measures can be a bit misleading in the context of an insurance company portfolio.

NOTE 9-4

Bob has simplified many things for his current audience as he prepares for his evening class presentation, but there really is a lot more even to the apparently simple calculation of total return.

When reviewing total return performance, we first must understand how the return was calculated. You might think this is as simple can be, but the accepted rules for such calculations can be found in the CFA Institute's Global Investment Performance Standards (GIPS) again. The general rule is that such returns should be time weighted and not be subject to different results depending upon the timing of cash flows into or out of the investment portfolio.

Once we are in agreement as to how performance is calculated, we should start making reasonable adjustments to the calculation. First, total return should be looked at after manager fees and, of course, against relevant benchmarks. We discussed those benchmarks back in Chapter 6. But when comparing performance of an active manager to a passive benchmark, what we are really doing is asking the question, "How do my manager's results compare to a passive alternative?"

Since passive alternatives provide for very low fees, one adjustment that should be made to the manager's total return is the investment management fee. In other words, the manager achieved the return of 'x' but it cost us 'y' for this result.

NOTE 9-4

In addition, for taxable entities like most insurers, there should be a calculation of after tax performance as compared to the passive alternative.

To calculate after tax performance, the total return number is adjusted by the amount of accrued taxes that would be paid or refunded (in the case of a loss). The accrued taxes are calculated on investment income and realized gains and losses. Typically, the company's highest marginal tax rate is used in the calculation. This is approximately 34% for most insurers.

Of course, no adjustment can go without an exception. And, that is made for income from 'tax-exempt' or municipal bonds. One must carefully use the relevant tax impact for tax-exempt investment income, which will vary depending if the company is taxed as a property/casualty insurer or not. The general rule on tax-exempts is that there is little, if any, benefit from tax-exempt income for life insurers. Thus, life insurers seldom hold bonds paying such income. However, property/casualty insurers must add back part of the 'tax-exempt' income received, which results in a top marginal tax rate of about 5.1% on 'tax-exempt' income. Yes, the IRS has a way of collecting tax on income that is typically called 'tax-exempt'. Thankfully, they have not followed the accounting profession by calling such income "Other Than Tax Exempt," but time will tell.

NOTE 9-4

Thus, total return calculations should be time weighted and adjusted for manager fees and taxes, as applicable, with all calculations made according to GIPS.

And, if you've got more than one portfolio, the entire investment process' total return performance should be combined. First, by asset class (e.g. fixed income versus equities) and then on a combined portfolio basis.

Add a display of total returns in different time periods versus relevant benchmarks and you have got a pretty good snapshot of how the portfolio is doing with regards to total return.

Let's give Bob the benefit of the doubt on this. Let's say he has kindly kept things less complex for the benefit of his audiences. And, that returns during his watch were generally pretty good. How could that possibly contribute to his firing?

NOTE 9-5

Performance attribution is something that many investment managers will not volunteer, but should be required of any investment management relationship.

For fixed income, performance attribution should tell us to what extent decisions about the portfolio's duration, sectors and securities each impacted over or under performance. This is important, because most managers will tell you they try not to add value with interest rate decisions (duration) but by their decisions about what sectors (e.g. corporates, mortgage backed securities) to over or underweight versus the benchmark and what specific securities to buy within those sectors. Thus, if performance attribution results show that much of the over or under performance was due to duration, we have a disconnect between what the manager has told us and reality. Of course, since core fixed income total return is most usually impacted by duration decisions, it will be incumbent upon the manager to stay close to the benchmark, and most do so. Thus, we must be careful in setting the investment benchmark.

For equities, performance attribution is usually easier for the manager to calculate. It should tell us to what extent performance was due to general stock market moves, investments in certain industries or sectors or investment in certain securities within those industries or sectors. Once again, choosing the correct benchmark is quite important for us to get value from reviewing performance attribution results.

10

ONWARDS AND UPWARDS

"The mailman just came, Bob. I'll get it." Sue closed the front door behind her to keep in the dog while she walked down the path to collect their mail.

Bob heard the door close, cutting off her voice. He didn't catch what she said. He had been concentrating, revising his job application letter. His campaign included sending letters to chief financial officers of companies that weren't even advertising jobs.

What is it they say? At least half of all unfilled jobs are never posted. He leaned back in his swivel chair, linked his hands behind his head and thought of Sue. Their life together had not started off very well in that coffee shop, the scene of what might have been their first date. But they had made up for lost time after that. Bob had been just out of the Army and suddenly doubting the wisdom of his decision to chuck it; Sue, just out of a job and looking for something at least a tad better.

What they found was each other.

Ha! Bob caught himself laughing aloud just as Sue opened the door again, automatically pushing her foot in to keep Molly back. Bob registered the click of Sue's heels on the tiles. Suddenly she was standing in the door.

He asked, "Who's the lucky guy?"

"Huh?"

"High heels," he explained.

Sue flashed an enticing semaphore of mascara-dark lashes, just enough to stir casual carnal thoughts in a guy writing a job application. She had a way of leaning against the line of the doorframe that emphasized her waist and the curve of her hips. Now she offered, "Coffee with the girls," by way of explanation.

"Six sigma," he mused.

"Would you mind explaining that?"

"S-curve. Sinusoidal. Standard deviation in the population."

"Deviation?" Sue smiled. "Who's got sex on his mind again?" She advanced to Bob's desk and bent forward. He sat up. They kissed.

Lightly he held her loose strand of beads, keeping her down. "Mirror, mirror, on the wall, who's going to be tallest of them all in those heels?" he asked, his mouth at her ear.

"How 'bout we trade?" she responded. "You let me stand up and I'll give you a letter that came for you."

"Who from?"

"An insurance company."

"They probably want to insure us."

"It doesn't look like junk mail. Here," she said, handing over the envelope.

Bob took it, recognizing the company name immediately as one he had written to two weeks before. He could feel his anxiety level rising as he reached for the letter opener. He had already met too much rejection; or silence, and that was worse.

'Dear Mr. Short,' he read,

'Mr. Jeff Parr, our CFO, has asked me to respond to your letter of October 15, in which you apply for the position of Chief Investments Officer. Mr. Parr and several of his senior colleagues have reviewed your package of documentation and invite you to meet our interview panel. ... Please call me to set a mutually convenient time.

Sincerely,
Barbara Chisholm
Director, Human Resources
Wilsdorf Insurance Company

"What does it say? What does it say?" Sue, looking through the back of the paper, could only see that the text ran longer than usual on a rejection note."

Bob looked up, smiling. "They want me to come and see them!"

"Oh, Bob! I'm so happy for you."

"For us, Hon. And," he added, "may there be many more."

"More what?"

"Interviews!"

"Hey, don't spoil it, Bob. You'll ace it in one."

"Let's hope so," he told her. "But here's a puzzle."

"What's that?" Sue asked.

"When I get to sit across the table from these guys, this has got to be the first question out of somebody's mouth: Why did you leave your previous employer?"

Sue's smile faded. She said nothing for a while. Then, "Why don't you call your friend, Jeremy?"

"Honey, you always have the best ideas." Bob kissed her again for good measure. He didn't tell her he already intended to. "I've got everything else down pat. My stats are good..."

Sue interrupted, "They're the best! You said so yourself."

"But I could never get my head around that question, Sue:

UNCERTAIN TIMES | 215

Why did I leave those guys? Telling the interview panel, 'Because I was fired, or I had more sense than to stay,' just doesn't cut it."

"What else do you need?"

"Well, like I said, my track record is great. And I've got the right references."

"Including Jim Greening's? It's so *pro forma*, like a stamp in your passport."

"What else could that jackass say? At least it's positive. There's plenty better than that in my package."

"So," Sue was too eager to play Devil's Advocate, "when they ask why you left, what will you say?"

"Honey, we just covered that. I'll call Jeremy. Don't worry, Sue." Bob squeezed her hand. "You see, this'll go just fine."

Bob was beginning to recognize the interior of Jeremy Libertz's condo as if he lived there. This time he discovered the kitchen, as Jeremy poured him a scotch and asked, "Remind me. How much water d'you take, Bob?"

Bob, leaning on the countertop, replied, "I'm closer to the tap than you are, Jem. How 'bout I add it myself?"

"Yeah, go for it. Tap's not too elegant but, hey, if I filled a jug of Waterford Crystal to serve it, the water still comes from the same place."

Bob took his glass, adding, "Best not to think too many steps back along *that* supply chain!"

They laughed. Jeremy poured himself a seltzer and ushered his guest toward the sitting room. The chess set was not front and center this time. It sat on its little table at the side of the room.

"So, you got yourself an interview!" Jem's tone was flat, as if he had never doubted Bob's ability to get back in the race. "Wilsdorf Insurance. Medium-sized, family-run till recently. No frills, I'd say."

"No frills?"

"They run a tight ship. Straight down the middle of the road. They're bottom-line people. Not about to twist themselves in knots over bonuses they didn't earn."

Bob felt more comfortable.

"My best guess is they unrolled your stats down the boardroom table, took a long look, gave a long low whistle and came away pleased." Jem continued, "Of course, there's gamesmanship everywhere; just less of it at Wilsdorf. The family were German Quakers originally. The likes of Gordon Gecko didn't make 'em over—yet."

"You said, 'Gamesmanship'?" Bob was mystified.

"Tush, tush, Bob, what else didn't they teach you in officer school?" Jem sipped his seltzer and stretched his legs, determined to further Bob's education. "No wonder you got yourself fired. It's a British word. Who else? It's where you win the game with devious, but not exactly illegal, practices." Jem took another sip, speculating, "Males of the ruling class refined gamesmanship before they were out of their teens at those big boarding schools they have."

"Hmm," was all Bob could find by way of response.

"Then the guy who gave us 'gamesmanship' went on to give the world 'one-upmanship'! Of course, we Americans had to have a come-back that sounded simon pure. We settle for 'Office politics.'" It means the same. Just doesn't sound as nasty."

"Uh, O.K., and Wilsdorf ... ?

"Still a tidy ship, I hear. I bet they homed in on your bottom line."

"And nothing else?"

"Oh, hey, the human species is a social beast. Numbers alone don't cut it. They'll want to know you're an upright citizen who plays the game—a team player."

"Oh."

"You still don't get it, do you, Bob."

"What don't I get?"

"*Communications*, kiddo! You don't need numbers to ace this interview; you need a communications plan that'll knock 'em dead. You need to lead with that communications plan that tells them—without being indiscrete and mentioning bonuses, of course—that they'll be far out ahead when you spot something on your radar. You tell 'em how you intend to distribute your news, you tell 'em you'll huddle with the senior guys to decide that distribution, and you tell 'em what you'll tell them and how it fits with what they need to hear: plenty of warnings about future trends."

"Future trends, Jem? I'm not clairvoyant."

"They need someone who'll give them warnings in a timely manner."

"Right."

"Know what I mean by *timely*, Bob?"

"I think so."

"How 'bout *warnings*?"

"Makes sense."

Bob must have sounded dubious, naïve, or both, because Jem shot back, "Jeez, I told you earlier they're not about to twist themselves in knots over bonuses they didn't *earn*—but, they're not so American Gothic they don't give a toss about cash!"

"Gotcha!"

"I hope so, 'cause you sure hit the iceberg the last time around. Here's the metaphor you gotta project: A five minute *tsunami* warning is ten thousand times better than five seconds."

"Roger. Wilco!" Resorting to Army jargon produced the desired effect: Jem stopped speechless. For a few seconds anyway.

When he spoke again he was calmer. "O.K., kiddo," he started counting on his fingers, "You got a great hold on the subject. You got a great hold on the products. You got a great network. You got a good track-record in numbers. You got a great hold on the investment process in your lecture notes, from strategic asset allocation to performance measurement. You even understand the bond market! Feed 'em the buzz words. You got a great hold on, uh… What I mean is: What you don't know, you know where to look it up. Right?"

"Right, Jem."

"You gotta convince those guys that you, Bob Short, are the early warning system they don't know they're looking for, but that they need. If you do that, you won't be beat. The guys at the table will all be of a certain age: They watched those films in school on 'duck and cover.' That's what they want in tough times. Assurance. Lay out your communication plan, Bob—it's the only thing you're missing—and you got it made!"

"Except for one small thing, Jem."

"What's that?"

"If I'm so darn clever, Jem, why did I leave my last employer?"

"Oops, we didn't solve that. What do you have on paper?"

"A reference from Greening that's about as enthusiastic as cold spit."

Jeremy contemplated his empty glass. "Time for a refresher. I gotta think. More scotch, Bob?"

"Seltzer, please, Jem."

"Fine. I'll be right back."

Moments passed. Jeremy emerged from the kitchen with a glass in each hand clinking fresh ice. "It seems to me," he said, handing Bob his glass, "that your former friends hit a few bumps recently."

"Sure they did. There's a lot of it going around."

Jem contradicted him, "Oh, no, no, no. Their wounds right now are self-inflicted! Since you called me first, oh, three weeks ago, I made a point of following them. The ratings and the business pages have not been kind."

"Why should they be, Jem? The company took a dive."

"Why is that, Bob?"

"We were doing O.K. on the investment side. Our portfolio was pumping."

"Thanks to you! Oh, and you can forget that 'we.' It's 'them' now."

"Yeah. Well, the business itself took a hiccup or two. Still is. It'll take a long time to build their revenues again."

Jem asked, "How come?"

"You mentioned Gordon Gecko earlier. The guys who took us over had that mindset. They thought they'd raise margins by saving commissions: they cut loose a few agencies."

"The best and the brightest?"

"The ones who delivered—and charged accordingly."

"Let me guess: that was supposed to boost the company's profit line for a quick flip."

"They played their cards close to their chest, but those were the vibes we got."

Jem clinked his ice and took a sip. "I guess they hadn't figured that recruiting insurance customers is a local, grass-roots industry…"

"… and the grass grows slowly," Bob added.

"Hey," said Jem, "Guys like your takeover champs don't care squat for regional and small-town agencies that build customer networks through three generations. Was Greening one of the new brooms?"

"No. He just had his fingers in the air to know which way the wind blew."

"So," said Jem. "There's your answer to that aggravating question: 'Mr. Short, why did you leave your previous employer?'"

Bob agreed, "Yep!" enthusiastically. "Company gets taken over; subsequent actions by new management clearly designed to raise profit margin for quick flip but results in damage to the core business in the worst recession in seventy years; …"

Jem corrected him, "Make that eighty years."

"O.K., eighty! There were cuts coming in the company…"

"So, pro-active as ever, Bob, you did not wish to contribute to the damage to an old, respected company."

"Uh, something like that, Jem."

"So you threw off the chains that held you to a sinking ship."

"I did?"

Jem raised his eyebrows, looking pityingly at Bob before nodding a few times silently. Bob took the hint.

"Right on, Jem. A guy's gotta be proactive in these times."

Jem coached him again, "There were cuts coming."

"There were, actually. I got advance warning, indirectly. A few weeks before they kicked me out they asked me to find extra cash in the portfolio…"

"Let me guess. For severance packages!"

"They didn't say, Jem, but…"

"The writing was on the wall."

"Yeah."

"My advice to you, Bob, is to write down that little sequence of events, hone it down, remove all personal animus, write it over and over again till it's crystal clear and learn what's left by heart like it was your elevator speech."

"You think that does it, Jem?"

"Ain't nothing better, kiddo. Their present troubles are a matter of public record, and your loyalty to business ethics, not to mention your timing—Impeccable!"

Next morning Bob Short slept in.

"Are you O.K., Bob?"

"Never better, Sue. At least, never better these past few weeks. I learned a lot from Jem last night."

"Want to tell me?"

"Sure." He gave her the short version. Then, "Let me get up and get dressed. We can talk it through later."

Downstairs they did just that. Bob recounted the evening before, thought by thought, if not word for word. As he sat in their kitchen reporting Jem's advice he rejoiced silently as Sue's mood improved. It had started with his first positive report when he got home.

She was wearing a long, clinging Donald Davies dress in Irish wool dyed two tones of orange. Of course it was clingy: natural wool did that. Long-waisted. Very retro. Very chic. In easier times Sue had bought several of that designer's dresses. In primary colors. She knew how to compete in a crowd. Sitting in their kitchen, describing his evening with Jem, Bob had new eyes for his wife: it took nerve to go to a dress-up occasion wearing a forty-year-old designer dress and carry it off as a social coup: 'Oh, this old thing. I got it at a charity store.' Maybe they would build up their social circle again—when he got a job.

With difficulty Bob pulled his head away from mind-chatter and back to the point in hand. "So," he told her, "I'm going to write up my notes, cover the angles I missed before, and at least I'll be prepared."

And he would take a lesson from his wife and be more competitive, too."

That took shape with his first scribbled lines on his yellow pad:

~ A Communications Strategy ~
Establishing a network for timely warnings
to alert key personnel to changing market conditions.

Based on practical applications
of U.S. Army communication protocols in combat

Sue came in, Sue went out; Molly came in, found herself ignored and took herself off to find better company. Bob worked through the day, never stopping, developing his strategy until he reached the point where he was satisfied: he would only have to tweak a few words the next day.

Then it was time for that 'elevator speech' Jem had mentioned. That took maybe half a day, a great investment in time. Days passed. Bob refined his words, reciting the product like a mantra.

On the day of the interview Sue bundled their baby into her car seat and drove Bob downtown.

"How are you feeling?" she asked for the third or fourth time.

"As good as I was when you asked me before," he told her, smiling.

"I'm more nervous than you are," she confessed.

"That may be. Me? I'm mellow. Unless there's a left field I haven't discovered, there's no question can phase me that comes out of left field," he told her, adding, "If that makes sense."

The last thing Bob saw of his wife that morning was Sue's reflection in the glass of the revolving door of the tower housing Wilsdorf's offices. She was waving from the open window of their car. He stopped in the lobby, confident, turned and waved back.

11

EPILOGUE

Bob Short is one of the lucky ones. Although fired from his job, he was able to carefully think through what he had done and how he had performed on his previous job. The answer was, on the surface, a simple one. Senior management, and indeed the rest of the company, had bonuses tied to pretax income, yet Bob, as CIO, had incentive compensation based upon beating investment benchmarks.

When things were going well, there was little in the way of dissonance between the two goals. However, earnings slumped, especially due to credit losses, while total return investment performance exceeded benchmarks, and severe dissonance occurred. And, it was the kind of dissonance that a silo-based organization could only handle by finding the cause, and firing the individual responsible for the losses.

Was this insurer's decision fair? Of course not. But, seldom are such decisions completely fair, since they have a political element to them.

"Why was I fired?" is one question that, many times, is never adequately answered. And, perhaps in this case, Bob discovered one of only several true answers. More importantly, he enters his new position, if he gets it, a little wiser and a little more appreciative of how to develop a successful investment process for an insurer.

But, like Bob, we must remember that developing a successful investment process for an insurer is an ongoing process. Financial markets, the business of insurance, regulations, rating agency biases, accounting regulations and other factors are always changing. Being aware and managing that change is part and parcel of both improving and monitoring the investment process of an insurer.

During uncertain times, this will continue to be a challenge for all insurers and their Chief Investment Officers.

INDEX

A

A.M. Best, 66
actuaries, 25, 39
admitted assets, 92
analytical reporting review, 157
asset/liability management, 38, 39, 177

B

BCAR, 66
benchmark, 12, 26, 50, 60, 61, 71, 105, 107-114, 117-126, 130, 136, 137, 150, 152, 169, 170, 189, 192, 193, 207, 209, 211, 212, 225
black swan event, 160, 193
board of directors, 9, 39, 46, 51

C

capital gain, 94
cash-flow, 15, 18, 25, 44, 45
claims, 7, 15, 17, 34, 44, 45, 158
conflicts of interest, 198
convexity, 63, 75, 120, 130
core fixed-income manager, 140
corporate bonds, 64, 74, 109
credit risk, 42, 47, 69, 97, 101, 103, 120, 173, 174, 175, 198, 199, 200
customized benchmark, 61, 120, 121, 124

D

default, 9, 74, 159, 162, 174, 199, 200
deleveraging, 69
derivatives, 169
due diligence, 70, 147

duration, 32, 40-42, 44, 45, 47, 60, 63, 66, 72, 75, 82, 97, 101, 110, 120, 121, 124, 125, 212
Dynamic Financial Analysis, 39, 63

F

fair value, 9, 73, 179
fixed income, 8, 9, 35, 42, 94, 97, 103, 108, 109, 111, 120, 124, 125, 149, 194, 201, 211, 212

G

GAAP, 200, 201, 202, 205
GIPS, 209, 211

H

hidden risk, 198

I

impairments, 8, 126, 204
incentive compensation, 26, 225
index fund, 118
Information Ratio, 185, 207
interest rate risk, 41, 120
internal ratings, 174
investment consultant, 142, 147, 207
investment income, 8, 41, 42, 43, 50, 66, 92, 94, 97, 107, 122, 184, 192, 198, 199, 202, 210

investment manager, 80, 86, 107, 109, 118, 119, 121, 122, 124, 140, 141, 142, 148, 151, 156, 169, 171, 174, 175, 176, 208, 212
investment policy, 51, 59-63, 70, 72, 76, 156, 169, 173
investment strategy, 38, 51, 119, 120, 165, 179

K

Key Performance Indicator, 8, 50

L

leverage, 30, 99, 101, 162
liquidity risk, 120
long tails, 44

M

manager search process, 143
manager selection, 71, 141
mark to market, 9
marketing group, 26
mortgage-backed securities, 9, 75, 109
municipal bonds, 210

N

NAIC, 200

O

Other Than Temporary Impairment, 73, 92, 179, 184, 204

P

performance attribution, 193, 194, 212
policyholders, 7, 26, 32, 58
portfolio monitoring, 71, 154, 168
premiums, 17, 44, 45
Pugh Matrix, 142, 143, 144, 146

R

rating agencies, 69, 74, 157, 173, 199
rating agency, 119, 174, 199
realized gain, 201
realized loss, 7, 43, 199, 201
reserve adequacy, 25
reserves, 7, 32, 35, 40, 41, 44, 45
return on assets, 92
risk appetite, 27, 43, 47, 50, 51, 53, 56, 66, 67, 72, 74, 76, 101, 156, 161
risk management, 27, 38, 62, 119, 157, 161, 177
risk/reward, 27, 47, 50, 119

S

S&P 500, 49, 123
senior management, 9, 26, 27, 28, 38, 39, 42, 43, 46, 50, 51, 67, 71, 74, 119, 122, 150, 151, 184, 197
severity of loss, 74
Sharpe Ratio, 207
silo-based organization, 25, 225
standard deviation, 49, 193, 207
STAT, 14, 15, 33, 35, 39, 40, 43, 58, 63, 70, 71, 73, 74, 76, 80, 81, 82, 83, 86, 90, 99, 128, 131, 137, 144, 150, 157, 158, 159, 162, 164, 165, 174, 179, 182, 183, 187, 191, 193, 199, 200, 201, 202, 204, 205, 213, 215, 217
Strategic Asset Alliance, 6
strategic asset allocation, 29, 31, 38, 51, 62, 110, 124, 125
stress test, 62, 177
surplus, 8, 35, 38, 41, 47, 49, 50, 66, 99, 101, 119, 183, 202
surplus optimization, 47, 49, 50
surplus portfolio, 47

T

TBAs, 169
total return, 7, 8, 26, 41, 49, 50, 71, 81, 107, 120, 122, 123, 126, 184, 185, 186, 200, 202, 206, 207, 209, 211, 212, 225
treasuries, 97, 101, 108, 109, 110, 120, 124, 130, 136, 205

U

unrealized gain, 201
unrealized loss, 43, 201
US treasury bills, 71, 169

Y

yield, 7, 8, 26, 40, 41, 42, 60, 64, 71, 75, 81, 82, 84, 85, 86, 94, 95, 97, 101, 103, 107, 108, 111, 112, 120-125, 133, 171, 172, 182, 183, 184, 186, 193, 194, 198, 199, 200, 202, 206
yield-based benchmark, 121, 122

Made in the USA
Lexington, KY
05 January 2010